ATOMIC BALMS AND OTHER WEAPONS OF MASS SALVATION

(Ruminations on the Human Condition, Life Contradictions, and Other Stuff)

By

Bonita Y. McCall

L'Edge Press
PO Box 1652
Boone, NC 28607
ledgepress@gmail.com

For

JEANETTA McPHERSON SWINNEY

(The first true friend)

And in Memory of

My Incredibly Wonderful Siblings,

STEPHEN IV, ROCHELLE, and BRANDON

ACKNOWLEDGEMENTS

First and foremost I give honor, praise, and thanksgiving to God for constant blessings and for my extraordinary life.

I am deeply grateful to my son, Evan, for his brilliant suggestions and for his uncanny way of keeping me always steered toward the heart of the matter with love, gentleness, and a zany sense of humor.

I give thanks, with all my heart, to wonderful friends and extended family for their inspiration and encouragement: Jeanetta Swinney, Gloria K. Smart, Clare Bernatsky, Alphonoso Carter, Gloria Martinez, Debra Iyanu Randall, Phyllis Brashear, Willa Short, Ernestine Washington, Dyanne Elzia, Audrey Johnson, Dr. Susan Cavallo, Charlotte Suber, Lizz Harris, Erma Denter, Rev. Dr. Jeremiah A. Wright Jr., Anna Hicks, "Bo" Hendley, Louis G. Blache, Ma Nawili G., Debra Bures Grigsby, and Helene Montgomery.

Each of you has given me your special brand of insight and unflagging support for my artistic endeavors. You have shared your time, your strengths, your patience, your humor, and your love. Your caring makes me a spiritually wealthy woman and a better human being.

Deepest appreciation to Jeff Hendley, publisher exemplar, who goes above and beyond for all authors fortunate enough to be in his literary care.

Thank you Abbie, for your wonderful, detailed graphics, creativity, and for basically putting this book together!

A very special thank you to Chamon Gayton for making the book cover a work of art!

CONTENTS

FOREWARD

Bonita McCall: Artist and Activist, Poet and Prophet

Bonita McCall's gift for punning and rhyming is evident from the title and sub-title of her book: ATOMIC BALMS AND OTHER WEAPONS OF MASS SALVATION (Ruminations on the Human Condition, Life Contradictions, and Other Stuff). If the first alludes to the central thesis of the book—that only love can redeem us—the second is a prelude to the miscellaneous character of the collection. At first glance, prayers, poems, memoirs, essays, political satire, short stories and fables tumble each after another, haphazardly. It is only at the book's end that the reader realizes that the order is anything but random.

McCall's table of contents reveals another aspect of her creativity: it is simultaneously retrospective and anticipatory, celebrating the elders of African American culture, especially her foremothers, while anticipating, in some cases, by more than three decades the most audacious assertions of New Age spirituality, and the most recent experiments in verse form, such as the poetry slam, rap and hip hop. It could hardly be otherwise for this daughter of a multi-talented family. Bonita's brother, the late, great Steve McCall, as musicians so often call him, was one of the pioneers of the Free Jazz movement, as well as the co-founder of The Association for the Advancement of Creative Musicians. In fact, this year, 2015, is the 50th Anniversary of this seminal organization, AACM, which brought excellence in music, the most advanced techniques in pedagogy, and universal access to education to the children of Chicago's Black community.

Bonita McCall's sister, Rochelle Grace Toyozumi, named after her grandmother Grace B. Scott, took up Grace's ministry with the lock-down population, developing for Chicago's Safer Foundation, a comprehensive education program for ex-offenders that boasted one of the lowest rates of recidivism in the state of Illinois. At the same time, like her sister Bonita, a gifted pianist, dancer, writer and storyteller herself, Rochelle was also an artist, inheriting her mother's fine voice, singing back-up during the 60's at Chess Records and gospel in the church choir at the family's beloved place of worship, TUCC, Trinity United Church of Christ (Pastor Emeritus, Reverend Dr. Jeremiah Alvesta Wright, Jr.). This love of music came naturally to all three siblings from their mother, Willa Brown McCall, who possessed a beautiful coloratura voice, singing as a girl with "Professor Mundy's Choral Ensemble."

From the first time I entered their lives in the fall of 1971 while studying for my PhD at the University of Chicago, I thought that a book should be written just simply about this extraordinary family, gifted practitioners of the arts, unsung patricians of my city, who, at the time, were committed to their community, the celebration of its African roots, and their unwavering belief in the Christian message. That last was the legacy of their grand-mother Grace, who taught her daughter and grand-children love of others, regardless of race, creed, color, or rap sheet. Indeed, Grace taught Bible in some of the city's poorest neigh-borhoods and most harrowing prisons. I remember Christmas when her former charges, now upstanding farmers and business people, would arrive at the McCall home with a whole slaughtered cow for the family, so that Grace would have choice meat throughout the cold winter months.

These, then, are Bonita McCall's roots: a strong family with deep spirituality, a com-mitment to community service, and a jubilant celebration of music, especially jazz. Unfor-tunately, the world she grew up in was not a mirror of her household. Born in the poverty and rigid segregation of the 30s, reared in the 40s and 50s where Jim Crow racism was still the norm, even in the North, Bonita McCall knew prejudice and want; but fortunately for her readers, these were not her only defining experiences. McCall came of age in the painful, turbulent, yet hope-filled days of the civil rights movement, and its concomitant flowering in the arts, the Black Arts movement of the 1960s. All of these happenings are reflected in the kaleidoscopic fashion in Atomic Balms. All of these changes are registered in its mainly chronological pages. Not only the self-transformation of the writer, which is continuous and includes all of McCall's diverse personae, but the molting of society's many layers, from the ubiquitous racism of her childhood to the resurgence of a proud African American iden-tity that is not only racial but also gendered. Thus, many of these poems pay tribute to the Black woman – Abbey Lincoln, Maya Angelou, Rosa Parks, even the dreaded figure of "Sap-phire," whom McCall rehabilitates in one of her lyrics as "a woman in all ways… stalwart in keeping light/Ablaze."

Then there are the poems that pay homage to other artists, or play on other tradi-tions: Langston Hughes and haiku, a Beatle's tune playfully glossed, or a play on words using the acronym for the Young Man's Christian Association for its penultimate line: "Yo Momma Can't Advance." With customary wit that never becomes bitter, even when it is implicitly recriminatory, the final line of the poem is nonetheless devastating: "(I knew I would get it sooner or later.)".

In McCall's envoi to the reader, she echoes her prologue, laying bare the ultimately simple message of Atomic Balms: only love can save us, a love that is universal, communal, and all-encompassing. Self-acceptance is the first step for this love, for it leads to love of self. Forgiveness is its necessary corollary, for it leads to love of others. Calling to our mind the picture of our planet Earth taken from outer space, she concludes with this exquisite, so very human, line: "We are part of this living vessel—this sailing ship of saints and fools and other evolving souls." Like the traditional Negro spiritual, "A Balm in Gilead," which serves as the epigraph to McCall's book, love is the most potent weapon, for it will lead to mass salvation; it is the atomic balm that "heals the sin-sick soul."

Susana Cavallo

Loyola University Chicago

PROLOGUE

A Balm in Gilead

"There is a balm in Gilead,

To make the wounded whole;

There is a balm in Gilead,

To heal the sin-sick soul."

(old "Negro" spiritual)

Being an "Atomic Balm" is living ones' life as part of the solution that not only helps solve humanity's problems, but also helps to heal the disease of divisionism that would destroy Earth.

At this dawning and awakening of our collective consciousness, all humanity is in the throes of birthing a new way to live on Earth by choosing life and peace over global suicide.

The journey to collective awakening begins with each individual confronting the mirror of self-acceptance, and learning to navigate the divine bridge of forgiveness. Since every one of us is a unique soul, our journeys are also unique and progress without time limitations. Some of us reach higher levels of consciousness before others, but those "others" may join in the positivity of global healing through agreement with the gut-feeling of sheer knowing without the experience of being there—yet!

By the way, the balm of Gilead, a tree common to the Middle-East and parts of North America, is characteristic by its heart-shaped leaves!

AUNT ELDER'S STORY

(On Becoming an Atomic Balm)

For one week I took part in non-violent, sit-in training. Dr. Martin Luther King, Jr. had come to Chicago and I had marched with throngs of "had enough of this unrighteous stuff" citizens.

I signed up to help integrate "Rainbow Beach", a segregated swimming area on a south-side stretch of "The Lake." It was not the best beach along the shores of Lake Michigan in my estimation. My friends and I preferred 57th Street beach, across the street from the Museum of Science and Industry and beautiful Jackson Park.

Rainbow Beach was in direct approximation of a nearly all black community, settled that way of recent times due to a mass exodus of white residents opposed to desegregation in housing as well as schools, churches, and any other form of togetherness outside the confines of their own skin type and way to thinking.

Although Chicago, Illinois is a part of the northern United States, Dr. King and many other "outsiders" had found (much to their amazement) that this city was more segregated and full of prejudice against its darker-skinned citizenry than many (so-called) notoriously hateful southern municipalities.

In training, being jostled, called a "Nigger" and other nasty names, or being spat upon, was intense, but being within the safe confines of our training facility and the camaraderie of our instructors and the other volunteers, I felt a new strength of dedication, inspiration, and racial pride. However, we were constantly reminded to stay aware of the moment and not to lose sight of the purpose of our non-violent participation.

One of the lessons we practiced was compassion and love for our tormentors; this was (and is) the conduit of fearlessness. Although fear may accompany the actuality of a sit-in, we were gently urged to remember that while we were going to be attacked by haters, sometimes viciously, we had to remain as calm as possible and to ***definitely not*** retaliate in kind!

My first participation in a real non-violent sit-in was at Rainbow Beach. The name-calling and being cursed at left me cool as a cucumber, but when this teenaged, white boy spit on me, I jumped up in automatic reactionary fury, totally forgot all non-violence training, and hit him in the mouth so fast it shocked him and me! I was a disgrace and I felt immediate shame.

In the confusion that followed, my older brother appeared out of the blue and was at my side. He grabbed my arm and quickly steered me safely away from the beach. I had no idea that he was even there, but I was not surprised that knowing my plans and knowing me, he might be there to cover my back.

A year later I tried non-violent training again. This time I paid closer attention to the philosophy of non-violence and the suggested methods of silent prayer or using mantras to block out the negativity spewed upon us during civil rights demonstrations. This next civil rights march and sit-in would take place away from Chicago. It would be in the South. There were long hours of training and even longer hours riding in chartered buses. It was summer and the roads were hot and dusty. The warm air coming in opened windows was dry and born only by the movement of the bus. When we stopped occasionally, there was no wind. We volunteers were full of enthusiasm and we sang many songs of hope until we became a bunch of weary sleepy-heads.

Of course the whole thing is still a surreal memory as I write about it some 40 years later, but some realities continuously regale the senses in a glorious sensation of light. Time has little to do with the effect of these singular realities and leaves one breathless with awe, understanding, and a kind of delight that memory cannot dim—even forty years later!

At that time, however, the whole world was in a state of flux, especially the United States. It was 1964, and the country was reeling in disbelief and horror after the assassination of President John F. Kennedy. The brief, but sincere, moratorium taken by the civil rights workers had led to a more concerted effort for positive change.

It didn't take long, after we arrived at our destination, for the scene to turn ugly and far more vicious than any training had prepared me. I felt fear all over. There was cursing, yelling, and "N"-words flying about that I'd never heard before. Every now and then a rock or other missile whizzed by. Some of us could not possibly keep still, as we had been instructed, because we were being jostled about by angry hands. The police did their duties in a half-assed way and their faces portrayed absolute hate for us. They were definitely not there to protect us.

In the midst of this chaos our leader called for prayer. We sat close to one another in cross-legged positions and we bowed our heads. Suddenly a wad of spit smacked my cheek and I raised my head to find a young man's contorted face within a breath's distance from mine. He screamed ugly words at me and spit on me again. In a flash time seemed to warp and I felt a rush of love for this wildly animated white man. An indescribable thrill rose in me like a full moon pulling the ocean's tide to shore. All I could think was "Dr. King was right! Dr. King was right!" I started smiling a huge smile of spiritual gratitude. I was experiencing a new depth of love and I was convinced this understanding was like a special gift to me from love itself! I was never so calm in all my life! I looked directly into the angry blue eyes of my tormentor and sent him pure love from my heart. He stopped dead in his tracks and wonder of wonders, he recoiled as though I had struck him and he actually ran away!! I watched him push through the crowd without looking back once! Then I knew, without a doubt, how Jesus felt when he prayed to God to forgive His tormentors because He knew they didn't have a clue what they were doing, not only to Him, but to themselves! And so, in that moment of truth and clarity I also uttered those profound words: "Father, forgive them. They know not what they do." Then I added, "They don't even know that they don't know!"

Many years later, when the civil rights movement became a platform for other injustices such as women's liberation and ending the Viet Nam war; when our neighborhoods were flooded with temporarily free dope and the little progress of human rights—with black children being escorted to newly unrestricted schools by the National Guard—a new part of history was rising in horrific view as the true aim of human rights began to deteriorate.

The assassinations of Dr. King, the Kennedy brothers, Malcolm X (whom many of us had just begun to appreciate beyond the media projection), of Medgar Evers, added to the various lynching of civil rights workers, and the murder of four little girls bombed to death as they attended Sunday school; these horrors, happening in the so-called greatest country in the civilized world, scrambled our senses like eggs on a grease-popping grill! As these ugly events were drilled into our heads many of us lost hope.

The black community was torn about the positive works of the Black Panther party and only seemed to become aware of their potential as great protective leaders after Fred Hampton was murdered in his bed. It was a time of a desperate unraveling of all but the most tightly knitted organizations—those with the least power to dismantle a government bent on keeping its citizens divided and treated unfairly except when it came to paying taxes.

America had become a super-power, feared and respected all over the world. The eyes of the Earth were fixed on this great country and many, who had found much to admire about the United States, now began to reassess their beliefs. The assassinations and vicious maltreatment of African Americans, as well as the calculated character assassinations of those whites who dared to challenge the prevailing governments "blind eye" approach to civil unrest and human rights, took a toll on the whole world. And while necessary anxiety was no stranger to the black community, it was the beginning of the Age of Orbital Stress throughout the globe.

In just a blink in time I found my old neighborhood an unfamiliar, even threatening place, but my new resolve to remain hopeful and spiritually aware gave me a certain peace.

I had to pass some brothers on the corner one evening. I felt instant pause. Gone were the days of relief in a woman who found herself alone and facing a group of young blacks. All the "black is beautiful" days were bye-bye. Black women were straightening their hair and wigging it down like never before! Black youth were ganging up in mostly illiterate groups, selling the no-longer-free-dope to their brothers and sisters and their out-of-work fathers and mothers as they also warred for turf and a ride in a hearse. Like China under British rule of yore, America was getting ready to sleep the drugged sleep of the spiritually broken.

I slowed my gait, but I continued moving toward the brothers who were animated in conversation. I only had six dollars to my name—another sign of the times—but I was suddenly overwhelmingly tired. I was not about to give up my last six dollars or be bullied by anybody! I had reached my limit. I was Rosa Parks tired.

I couldn't see any way around those boys and there was no one else on the block. I began to walk faster, in a "best-not-mess-with-me" kind of way. I held my head high looking straight ahead, but I could now hear their conversation. The very weight of their words made my feet come to a halt.

"…Man, I'm tired!"

"…Me too, Bro. I'm sick of this so-called system!"

And from a third, "I can't hang with all the shit out here. I mean I ain't nevah been this drugged. Ain't no jobs out here, period!! This is some tired shit!"

My feet turned around on their own recognizance. My mouth flew open as brain, heart, and soul all merged in too real an understanding.

"TIRED!?" Oh Lord, was I screaming!? I didn't mean to.

"When was the last time you layed-in, sat-in, prayed-in, trying to right an injustice, only to have crazed men with water-hoses on full force push your butt down the street ***so hard*** that the next time you were ABLE to make love again your hips sported scars!? I call 'em the scars and stripes forever; abrasive reminders from scraping up an Alabama street!?"

By now I couldn't stop myself. My hands seemed to be smoothing my skirt, but they were soothing the remembered wounds under the skirt. I was on fire. The gang of boys seemed frozen by my outburst. My voice was unrecognizable to me. It had become a whispered scream.

"TIRED!?

"Oh! From being on your knees, head bowed in the strength of prayer so powerful you had neither fear nor hate in your heart as you waited in front of a jail for Dr. King's release while the spit from Earth's enemy ran down the side of your face!?

"No, no, no…don't get me wrong! I am not trying to tell you to apologize for being a baby twenty years ago! Maybe you weren't even born. I am not asking you to re-establish those tried and true methods from way back then; methods so wonderful that here we are, all these years later, listening to Dan Rather-be-doing-something-else telling us that the government of the people is still working on the civil rights amended, statutory raped, amendment!

"No, young brothers, I would not insult you that way. But, if you're really ready to give up, give up your hair-net, pull up your pants, surrender your little pink curlers, hang up your doo-rag, 'cause that's more tired than you'll ever be in your entire life! Besides, it ain't about hair or a fashion mistake!

"Give up using weapons on yourself and against your own community. Take the fight where it belongs. Give up abusing yourself by killing your future for temporary pleasure. Realize the fact that when you initiate membership in a gang by killing your own black brothers and sisters, you instantly become welcomed slaves of a Ku Klux Klan mentality!"

I took a deep breath. I felt like I had been running a marathon. There was some shifting of feet and incredulous looks exchanged. The closest boy took a step toward me and spoke up: "We ain't kilt nobody! What you talkin' 'bout?"

"Just listen", I said. "If you're really, really tired I won't even ask you to think about the way to remedy the situation that makes you tired. I'll give you the answer, pure and simple, for free. Dick Gregory already gave us the solution a long time ago. I only need you to tell me what it is that you want.

"Jobs? Okay, but be specific and insistent. Tell the corporate world you need employment, but you need that employment offered with on-the-job-training and pay as you learn and until you get that you won't buy another bottle of whiskey, beer, wine, or tequila to salsa by!

"Better education for our children? Good! But let's make it better than that! Tell the powers that move the NEA, we want the SAME exact educational standards as the Lab School at the University of Chicago for all these little West side children and South side kids; the same high standards as Beverly Hills High for all the kids in Watts…and until we get that we won't buy another pound of pork in this entire nation! Let it be a smokeless, non-Bar-B-Q, non-labor day in America!

"Are you getting the picture? Do you see where I'm coming from? Do you see where you can go? You don't need no stinkin' gun! Old slick Unca' Sam is always delighted to see you coming out with your little pop pistols. He doesn't care how much you use them on your own and he would love you to threaten him with your little weapons for all the obvious reasons. He would love to nuke your little asses post haste!

"You do not need guns and violence to get your fair share of the economic pie. You do not need to sing to overcome injustice. You have powerful economic guns in your collective habits as well as your pockets. You don't have to march any more for your rights. You've been spending despair dollars on despicable dung that is doin' it to you to death.

"Keep your dollars in your pockets. Save your money for other enterprises and sit back in front of the television. Watch what happens. While you sit on your wallet, the hog barons and the whiskey merchants will be knocking each other down, out-lobbying one another to GET YOU WHAT YOU WANT!"

By now I had the boys' attention and some of them started to shake their heads in agreement and understanding. Some of them thought I was funny, but I was in the cone of a rocket ship fired off its launching pad and heading straight for their hearts!

"Do you really want to open some bureaucratic noses? Stop *sniffin' that coke!* Oh, don't hurt your selves! Just do it for one solid week on a collective front and you will blow this country out of its degenerative mind-set! (as Dick Gregory once reminded us).

"Leave Coca-Cola stewing in its own juices on the supermarket shelves! Don't eat or buy chicken for two weeks! Put the whole of society on notice just how tired you are!

"Now, if you're really sick and tired of a system that religiously kicks you when you're already down, and you want fair housing, or a fair medical plan that treats the poor with the same good medicine it prescribes for the rich—if you want fair anything—BOY-COTT CHRISTMAS!!

"Leave the evergreens forever in the forest! Give a child a much better gift, something you made with your own hands that came from your heart and tell that child about Jesus instead of some fat dude in a red suit! And the next time December twenty-five rolls around you'll have toys and presents delivered to your front door by reindeer-powered, chauffeur-driven limousines!! You'll be treated with low interest mortgages, decent housing, medical insurance, and bank loans will be falling in your laps.

"Always remember your economic power. You are the consumer, the buyer, the one who moves the merchandise. You are the biggest user of products and the biggest loser of cash and respect. But, we can only redistribute the wealth by working together. The whole world is one family, but we do not adhere to that truth yet. We can begin the process to a better world by becoming one family in our own communities. Togetherness is the key to improving our lot in this country and this world.

"I'm not telling you to do something I haven't tried. And I am not telling you this is something easy to do. Numbers help, intent helps, staying focused helps, and most of all, remembering that it can be done heaps helpings of blessed assistance on our collective consciousness.

"I gave up pork and honey, I still dream about ribs! I ain't got no smart electronics hanging off my belt and NOBODY loves music more than I do, but you see, I'm not buying any more toys until the Supreme Court kills bills for me! Oh yeah, I must admit I do like my wine. I confess I do. But it's MY WINE! I MASH MY OWN GRAPES! And sometimes I have to wait and wait and wait for it to be ready just like I'm waiting and waiting and waiting for you to really and truly get tired. You ain't tired yet!"

I was thoroughly spent as I walked away from those boys. I heard one utter a farewell: "Thanks Sister, take care." I also heard, "…You think she crazy?..." and "Where did all that shit come from?!"

What stayed with me from that encounter was the reference, "Sister". I was touched by that denotation that only a few years ago was a daily, non-flirtatious greeting in our neighborhoods. That utterance at this time was a sweet reminder more important than my perceived safety and for the moment I felt renewed fearlessness. Adam Clayton Powell's "Keep the faith, baby" rang like old good news in my recently tired, but now refreshed mind.

For all our achievements, our strides toward freedom, our incredible inventions, our remarkable art forms, our humor, and our abiding love, black folk were succumbing to old fears and new horrors even within our own communities. Chicago was becoming known, as in the 1920's, for gangs and murder and crime than it was for its beautiful lake and "big shoulders."

I am keenly aware that, as a whole, African-Americans are not normal people. We are a race of super-normal beings, healthier than the norm. Otherwise, our numbers would be more decimated than Native Americans by now. Otherwise we would not have the mysterious gift of innovation on so many fronts. We have overcome insidious poisons of many varieties aimed at killing us in wholesale groups beyond the mundane lynching and constant brain-washing of everyday injustices. After the end of legal slavery and "Reconstruction" we, as a race, were no longer needed or necessary in the minds of many of the movers and shakers that ruled the new country, now referred to as the United States of America. Willie P. Lynch had written a manifest promising that making a slave would last hundreds of years if done correctly. And now, as the 21st Century makes itself present, it appears that particularly peculiar racist knew something about the treacherous stain of lasting evil. I viewed black gangs, and the "dumbing-down" of Americans overall, as part of the Willie P. Lynch mentality on a roll. I could see my beautiful sun-kissed people returning to the lowest form of self-hate: obsessing over skin-color, "good hair", and a mad dash to own more things. I needed reassurance. I needed prayer. I had a talk with God.

POSITIVELY BLACK

(The Universality of Blackness)

One day

I asked in simple supplication of the wonder,

The why, the good, of my black skin?

How many the ways, the definitions, and man's damnation

This skin provokes, and seems to get

Under the skin

Of

So

Many

Hapless folks!?

And a voice spoke unto my heart:

Close your eyes.

Take a deep breath.

Now,

See the ewe

Of my lambs…

I am the power of pure outlets;

No plug nor socket here!

My open pores beget "black holes":

Quasars of uttermost mystery,

Oblivion's utterness,

And, as such,

The outermost industry.

I am the blueblackdrop upon whose bosom

Lay the stars, yea even your sun.

I cover the waterfront,

The depths,

And the electric candle in the lighthouse.

I am the tar in the pits of LaBrea

And the oil that spills over.

I am the black from whom all color

Springs into life,

Absorbing just enough light

In order to come back through me.

I am the black that every merchant dreams

To stay in.

I am basic, not only in your wardrobe,

But in your every waking moment.

Don't believe me!?

Just blink!

With every blink of the eye you come back to me,

And all day long you rush home.

My mother is the rest in your best sleep.

My father is sire of the entire Earth family-tree-roots.

My great-great-great grandchildren are your shadows.

I am the constant in all emergence and surrender.

But when (man) spoke

Darkness fell from his lips.

It covered the world in dire dis-ease

And un-happiness

And you became afraid.

So,

I gave you good nights

And black lights

And you danced

And you gave me romance.

You gave me romance

And moonsong.

In truth I enfold you…

Never to scold you…

Merely to hold you…

To love your trembling heart wide awake

Because

I am

Life's Oldest Vibrating Energy

And ewe, Christian soldier, are mine.

In the "Ah"-pealing silence that followed this clarion

I asked myself,

"Now is that black enough for 'ya!?"

And so it is.

ONE OF THOSE OPEN SECRETS

We are all born with two things in tow: Innocence and a warrior spirit. We are all warriors fighting overwhelming odds against our becoming the highest form of our unique selves. If only we would be taught, and then remember, that we come here winners; that we have already overcome tremendous odds just to be born. After all, did we not win the race to our mother's wombs, beating out millions of others to have the opportunity to become physically alive!? We are winners from inception to birth.

After we are born we go through a maze of obstacle courses: Mores, pretense, real love, reel love, all sorts of prejudice, truths, lies, and drains on our delicate emotions. We are coupled like box-cars, filled with training devices, that move us on rails of penalty tracks if we don't behave according to the status quo.

If we don't learn our personal reason for being, we suffer --even if we succeed on other levels. We all know in our basic gut, where we intuitively sense, that there is something missing when we don't achieve self-awareness. Even if we are deeply loved and nurtured, without self-acceptance and self-knowing, we cannot achieve true happiness or maturity. Without that basic key to our true identities, we are only wanderers living on the outskirts of our inner neighborhood.

It is the personal work of everyone's journey to find and then follow their "raison d'etre" (a leg on that trek which must be addressed) and it is generally impeded by so many hindrances—the greatest being survival. In other words, the more leisure one has, the more time one can use to find a personal dream and to discover one's main purpose for being alive. When one is hungry, questions other than where to find food are not relevant, but a simple meal can often be the catalyst for the inner search to begin. When one is starving for food, for love, for meaning, the same thing applies: Finding a way to slake the thirst that impedes the drive to physical, mental, or spiritual harmony. This is not to say that one has to be rich or have the luxury of vacationing in order to find time to focus on one's dream/purpose in life. Indeed, one only has to put the quest in thought-form as a request for fruition and one's path will be strewn with clues, as well as answers, along the way to self-discovery--no matter what circumstances one is in. The whole universe is in active favor for you to find your reason for being. To act in your favor, universal law only requires your willingness.

Self-acceptance is the key to harmony and the path to fulfillment. When we have this wonderful peace within ourselves; when we accept who we are—warts and all—we are able to give ourselves permission to do great things no matter where we may find ourselves in the world. Being poor or rich is a matter that has very little to do with money or things. No one is poor that accepts themselves for who they are. They realize a greater freedom beyond the snare of greener grass somewhere other than their own surrounding yards. They know that even though they do not have all the things that seem to be in vogue or worthy to others, they are possessed of the strength of non-attachment to things. They gain the wonder of forgiveness both for their own folly and for others. Forgiveness is one of the best balms on this planet and is sorely lacking among us.

Forgiveness is a must if we are to know peace within as well as outside ourselves. In the Christian world the "Lord's Prayer" is widely used in every church no matter the particular religion. It is a prayer usually repeated by the whole congregation at some point in the worship service.

This powerful prayer touches on every front necessary to the well-being of all who repeat it. Yet, I often wonder how many Christians really understand those words: "...Forgive us our trespasses as we forgive those who trespass against us..."? How many of us truly whisper that universal law in a real personal sense? When we pray and ask God to forgive us in the same way we forgive others and then go on harboring resentment for those who have aggrieved us, what have we done to ourselves? We have literally blocked the gift of forgiveness from being able to reach us! Prayer is one of the most powerful tools at our disposal and has the strength to take us through the terrifying times and over crucial impediments in our lives. It is part of universal law that anyone who implores God for help from their heart is not only heard, but given dispensation in God's time—not ours—and we only have to develop patience and faith to receive relief from our woe.

Often we expect immediate answers to our prayers and are disappointed when things seem to continue keeping us down or get even worse after we have prayed. God's time is completely different from ours. It is said that we operate on chronological time, but our Creator is beyond time and space and knows before we take our next breath the answers we need and when they are needed for our highest good. God only waits for us to come from sincere, prayerful hearts, but God must bless us and forgive us in the same way we forgive others. If "The Lord's Prayer" is your spiritual connection, be very careful that you do not block your blessings.

Every spiritual path orders our steps by faith and patience. These are ancient and time proven attributes worthy of every pilgrim, but in today's modernity faith and patience are not qualities much sought after. We are in a technological world heading for warp speed—the faster the better! But where are we headed in this competitive race against time and each other? It is like taking part in expensive technical games that yield cheap thrills and highs which dissipate as quickly as they are reached! The only thing that is apparently positive about all this incredible technology is the overwhelming exchange of information regarding the state of the world and how we can change it for the better. Collectively, in a way, we are reaching out to one another in a prayerful state of mind and I pray that we continue on that path through the internet as well as through meditative prayer done outside the physical world.

It may sound crass, stupid, or even ridiculous for me to suggest that forgiveness is tantamount to Earth's salvation, but I do suggest such a thing. No, I have not lost my children to murder. I have not suffered deprivation from living in a war-torn country, nor have I been through many of the evils of the world up close and personal. I do know, however, without a doubt, that this attribute (forgiveness) is the healing balm for almost all of our troubles. It is love's absolute balm.

I am part of a people that have a miserable history in the United States. We have been through accursed ills perpetrated by evil doers of practically every stripe, but we are some of the most forgiving human beings on this planet. For that I am proud, and know that this trait is representative of our super-normal character. Not all African-Americans share this wondrous state of being, however, and it isn't any wonder! But, an overabundant number of us do get on with our lives by forgiving, if not forgetting.

My first example of the power of forgiveness came, of course, from familial teachings. My parents, particularly my maternal grandmother, were deeply committed to Christianity. Jesus Christ's sacrifice on our behalf was taught to me and my siblings early on. I was very affected by the horror of the story of the crucifixion. For years I could not take my mind off the evil it must have taken for a group of people to do such a thing to another person. The vision of Jesus hanging on the cross stayed in my mind and haunted me and made me sad. But then the vision of my own people hanging from trees right here in America made me fully aware of how evil has pervaded this globe for eons.

As I got older, I concentrated more on Christian studies and visited many Christian churches of different paths. I got permission from my parents to visit churches of faiths different than mine and came to appreciate God by other names. There is no religion that I do not respect, but only Jesus came to Earth in order to redeem us from our sins through **forgiveness** and this revelation cast Jesus in a new light for me. Now Jesus no longer occupied that place on the cross in my mind. Now I felt His presence beside me as I made my way in life.

After much gnashing of teeth and guilt, I finally found the presence of mind and heart to forgive myself for my sins (both real and imagined). It had been relatively easy for me to forgive others, but try as I might I found it difficult to impossible to make my own self-forgiveness "stick." Finally, during an extraordinary journey to India I found grace. Then I began to see many instances where mankind, in modern times, had used the power of forgiveness to heal and grow by. I know that so many of us understand in our hearts that forgiveness is the correct way to live, but are too afraid to act on this principle because we have lost attachment to the umbilical cord of our warrior spirit. I still sin everyday, I imagine, either knowingly or unknowing, but though I am no saint, I do as Nelson Mandela once said and keep on trying.

When we forgive others we grow and we evolve. We become a blessing in the lives of others.

When we forgive ourselves we expand that evolution and receive the precious gift of being able to enjoy our own company.

When Dr. Martin Luther King, Jr. was stabbed by a deranged woman, he immediately asked his rescuers not to harm the woman who did this terrible thing to him.

I know that forgiveness is a "biggie" and not for the faint of heart, but as one wise author once pointed out, "God never promised us a rose garden."

My favorite definition of forgiveness comes from the prolific Anonymous: "Forgiveness is the scent of the violet on the heel that crushed it." How profound, this simple declaration!

A more recent example of the beauty and power of forgiveness came to us from the Amish community:

ODE TO THE AMISH

(A tribute to the Amish community in Lancaster County, PA for their calm equanimity on October 2, 2006.)

Gentle throwbacks from the future,

your presence stirs more ridicule

than not.

Simple ways in God-fearing plain nests,

you broke the shackles

that got

in the way of brotherhood

which others cleave to willingly,

allowing themselves to rush and run

toward tokens spun of gilded promise.

But you harness horses to power

your pace upon your place

on the land.

No race lures you into competition!

Your position is secure

by the Holy Spirit.

You find comfort by the hearth

which you take to heart

and there you rest today

in ways of olden golden praise.

I raise my hand to you this day

in solidarity and friendship

for your kinship

is a vessel sailing true in pure waters

running deep and steadfast

while others last themselves

to a past steeped in treachery;

wretches of repetition and greed,

but your needs found solace in giving;

living by a light

not found in electricity.

And when the madman

killed your little daughters

in order to kill himself,

you did not scream for revenge

nor rush to find some compensation.

Your dispensation came in hushed

and quiet prayer.

And there you found a strength

so uncommon

it cleaned the planet's clock

for one shocked moment in time.

You left behind your unhinged sorrow

and bound it up in forgiveness sublime

that found its way to page three

'cause

it wasn't headline news anymore.

(Heavens forbid the masses waking up via the media!)

Your act was relegated to way, way back

in the corner

in the storehouse of guilt,

not of madmen,

but of Judeo-Christian-Muslim-Hindu

folk of ordinary fears.

Your Christian understanding and integrity made the year

a blessed thing.

It made me take wing

like a J.L. Seagull

in rarefied air.

No outward fare proclaimed your response,

no medals nor honorable mention,

but the seeds of intention

from your mindful heart-set binds you to

an Earth in need of inheritors

who truly navigate a road less traversed;

one that only a great love unearths.

And then you nursed

a sick man's family with solace and care and hope

because you knew, deep down,

they would have to cope

with a world ready and waiting

to call names

and shame his kith and kin.

You squelched that low mentality

with a sacred one-two punch

wearing gloves so velvet

they caressed a new reality

into existence as sweet

as an Ali butterfly floating

in realms all around us.

I did not forget to breathe deeply

of the essence left in the wake

of your awareness.

I will never forget your lesson and the **balm**

of your remedy to hate.

It covers a bruised world's wounds

in a healing graced

by the mercy of our great

and very good God.

May those precious angels that you raised to saintliness

find their rest and heavenly play in the house of Jesus

for such is truly the kingdom of Heaven.

They did not cower in terror,

but asked that the killer shoot them first

because the smaller ones were scared.

And though he had no charity

for their super-conscious plea,

a clarity profound has spread its light

in sight

of every pulpit, prophet, and congregation

who proclaim themselves as righteous.

Your babies did not die in vain.

They did not die in vain.

"…and the meek shall inherit the Earth."

Forgiveness can come in many forms, but as we evolve into more civilized beings, this enlightened state is always preceded by mindfulness.

Note: Since the above occurred, televised interest in the Amish community has peaked. Several shows have focused on negative images of the Amish way of life – thus trying to diminish the magnificent gesture of communal forgiveness over such a heinous crime against them.

It is no coincidence. It is the "crabs in a barrel" mentality among the "puppet-masters." If we ever begin to forgive one another on a world-wide scale these "puppeteers" will lose control over us forever – and wouldn't that be something to behold and live by!?

A LITTLE ABOUT LA

(This incident may or may not be true.)

My friend is strong. She is my sister of the Holy Spirit *and* my friend. Our friendship goes all the way back to mud-pies, first lies, first truths, and lasting ties.

We were well into the second decade of ties that bind. Ten years plus, we had weathered many storms and, in turn, found ourselves anchors for one another as we plumbed life's depths. We shared our journey with the natural ease of connected seekers on the same path.

Then one fine day a moment of inscrutable clarity arose, defining my love and admiration for her as a woman, an authentic human being, a friend, and a true believer. It was the kind of singular incident that bleeds light through the confines of one's woodshed.

It happened at one of those grand parties; one of those seasonal bashes always accompanying and highlighting the afterglow of crowning successes, awarding high achievement in honorifics to super-terrific unique artisans. It was the kind of private and well-appointed affair that occurs after the television lights go dark and the winners let their collective hair down in after-after partying with Clio, Tony, Oscar, Obie, Grammy, Emmy, and "Dopey" all rubbing elbows and others body parts together in collective glee.

My friend "La", which is what I shall call her in this scribbling detail of a bright moment in our lives, was in her element, having been honored with a Clio for her creativity in the world of jingles and Madison Avenue. Besides that, she was one of the current darlings of high society since the dawning of her rise in the fast-paced orbit of commercial advertising. In point of fact, she exuded that sparkle, electricity, and super energy that fuels the currents of originality and interest. She was also a lot of fun to be with and known for her generous spirit.

There were other things she was known for too, like her "wild ways", her legendary love affairs, humanitarianism, and her latest personal project which was taking off in an orbit all its own—a book entitled, *A Journeyman's Guide For Youth Who Don't Wanna' Waste It*. And because people often dabble with the worse of themselves, there were some serious detractors among her many admirers and well wishers.

Missy (not her real name of course) was plagued by her own take on La. She respect-
ed La's obvious talents and her ability to live life on her own terms, but she found herself an-
noyed by the sense of unbridled freedom, seemingly inherent, in the good sister. Therefore,
the canvas Missy painted of La bore hues darker than the ebony skin of my friend who wore
it like a mahogany Amazon all up and down Madison Ave, Fifth Ave, Park Ave, 125th Street,
and other avenues in other cities—and La ain't all that tall physically!

The party was in full sway. Music poured over the guests like it was orchestrated for
each and every one present. It charged the atmosphere like a great Sunday morning sermon,
splintering a bucket of gut-busting blues into a fusion of rocking jazz and magnetic rhythm,
rhythm, rhythm.

La was enjoying a verbal tennis-match, a repartee as it were, with "Norm" (not his
real name either, and certainly anything but "normal!"). Norm had won a Clio two previous
years in a row. He was the first to predict a Clio in La's future. At that time it was early in her
career and she received wind of his sentiments with humility and a certain validation of her
peerage in the small, highly paid "think-pens" versifying attraction to everything on sale in
the world. New kids on the block rarely got attention on Madison Avenue with any immedi-
acy. The jingle probation was designed to jangle the nerves of the most talented newcomers
in a heart-breaking time-out. Most never made it to a corner office and were just happy to
get on a winning promotional team. La, not only got the corner office, but was among the
few ground-breaking persons-of-color in the ad world. These lucky few were quickly hired
by Madison Avenue execs during the dazzling rise of the civil rights movement. Being black
and a woman could have been tricky in the business arena. Big business was mainly cover-
ing its own big bottom-line and the hiring gesture did not also mean a change in attitude
with regard to race, gender, or the delineation of power. It was meant as a token thing, but
La slipped through the intention like an unexpected comet and made the company a lot of
"bottom-line." La balanced her work efforts with relish and with an uncanny understanding
of herself as a unique entity among all the other original souls inhabiting the same space.

Advertising goods and services was as old as history, but had reached an unparalleled
level of sophistication by the 20th Century. African-Americans (or Negroes as they were
deemed before late in the 20th Century) had been used (without permission) for ages in ads,
e.g. "Aunt Jemima" – pancakes; "uncle Ben" – rice; "The Gold Dust Twins" – Cleanser. It was
as though Madison Avenue spies hung around black communities just waiting for a new turn
of phrase to catch on. Slang "hooks" in language began to appear in commercials straight out
of the hood from "uptight" to "outta sight!" But no blacks were part of the jingle executive
world or the coveted Clio until around 1969.

La and Norm quickly developed a fast friendship that very often expressed itself in innocent, but rapid-fire faux flirtation based on verbal one-upmanship coupled with low-down signifyin' and mutual respect. Norm was also engaged to Missy and their wedding list boasted names that read like some kind of "in-crowd" who's-who.

I don't recall their banter that night at the party. I was not close enough to hear their exchange. I didn't need to hear it to still find myself enjoying the laughter from the crowd gathered around them. They were going at it like two consummate and devoted adversaries. They had been known to do this regularly although, as some would note later, never at a social event of this "outside the home turf" scale.

I was on my way to the garden, having just escaped the beguiling, but potentially dangerous clutches of a musical genius who had won five Grammy's last year, but who was also on-going salacious fodder for scandal magazines. I had just made it to the tall opened, beautifully etched glass and carved wooden doors that led to double balconies and over-looking the fabulous garden. Part of the garden had a tall maze of the greenest hedges I had ever seen. It seemed to invite one to get lost on purpose. I had promised myself to cherish this beautiful floral oasis one more time when a gale of laughter burst from the center of the room. I turned to its gleeful sound, now seeming to bounce off the walls. It was then that Missy's sobering voice rose loud and clear and accusingly: "La, don't you find it a bit strange to be riding on the crest of a book touting advice to the young about morals and making wise sexual choices when your own bedroom activities reportedly leave much to be desired?"

The hush that fell upon the room segued perfectly to a rest in the music and for a warped nanosecond only the evening birds in the garden could be heard. Then the music resumed and with it rustling whispers, nervous laughter, and instant movement. The guests became impromptu choreography shifting the gears of revelry.

This shift swept me along with it as I found myself rushing to the aid of my sister.

By the time I penetrated the edge of the closest people around La and Norm I saw a small parting of the crowd, allowing a slowly approaching Missy, her eyes intent on La. La seemed caught off-guard, her usually smiling face was a mask of surprise and frowns. She turned to face Missy, but it was Norm who suddenly grabbed my attention. He was standing there wide-eyed, slack-jawed, and frozen in place.

Later he told me that since everyone who mattered knew how devoted he was to Missy, including Missy herself as well as La, he couldn't imagine what provoked Missy to come "out of such a bag." He said that he simply couldn't process Missy's actions at first. After all we were all good to tolerant friends. There was a fair sized contingency of close friends from the ad world in attendance at this Bel Air gathering. This smaller group was constantly thrown together, mostly in celebration. And though they differed on occasion or completely disagreed with one another's ideas and/or lifestyles, they rarely made serious issues out of it.

Many times it was Missy, Norm, La, someone we can refer to as "Stick-Man", and me, having fun whittling words out of fertile imaginations. We would verbally wallow in debate about stuff, like the pulchritude of interpretation versus the beauty of truth or some other philosophical candy to munch on. We would deliberate in the most obtuse reasoning we could think of and we didn't miss a beat dancing, eating, laughing, while pretending to be serious.

Sometimes a whole new ad campaign got born at one of our "happenings." In those particular times much chaotic confusion would press around our ideas and would swirl through the gathering like an old star suddenly finding itself a nova. The new, successful, commercial spot contrived out of this play would usually not leave everyone happy who had been present at its birth, yet everyone there could be said to have fostered its beginnings in one way or another. But that's another story.

After that party Norm reflected how hard it was on Missy because of her faux pas. He had held her in his arms while she cried her heart out. He felt that he could honestly soothe her and coax her back to the best of herself. He said he could do this because early on in their relationship Missy had convinced him that she loved him warts and all. He said he believed no less in his feelings for her. Besides that he realized she had mixed her drinks at the party, experimenting with new and different tastes. Norm was convinced that the drinking contributed to her radical behavior. He also knew enough about La to trust all would eventually be well again among them. He just had to get Missy to forgive herself. I thought, "What a wise man!"

When I tore my attention away from the sight of Norm, my eyes fell on La. I moved to a spot where I could see her face and I saw that she was now smiling warmly. With that smile I shifted gears again, this time to the kind of neutral that had peace like a river flowing through it.

La's first words were edged in genuine disappointment, "Oh Missy…!" She gently shook her head and continued, "If you'd thought about it a bit longer, you could have answered your own question. You do have a point, and your question bears merit. I don't deny my romantic adventures which are more fiction than not, but in a way, perhaps, I'm a kind of every woman—real or imagined. You see, I've turned down more dick than most men even dream pussy is possible!"

This response was related in such a calm resonance that those straining to hear it couldn't possible mistake it as a nasty retort. And then Stick-Man threw up his hand and shouted: "Ain't that the truth!!" As heads turned toward Stick-Man, Betty Oak (not her real name and a promising Oscar nominee) delivered a resounding slap to the face of her husband! The band swung into a smooth version of Benny Golson's "Whisper Not" as both Missy and Betty O. hastily left the room, almost knocking one another down in the process. A hand grabbed mine and I found myself dancing in a cool bop with a very "cool", laughing stranger. I thought no moment in life could have been more surreal.

It was quite a scene. It took on a kinetic force that carried those within earshot through the next full week of dishing the dirt. However, it was not the special moment I grooved on and grew on. This happened three weeks later, well after the Clio awards and all the parties. La and I were traveling together on our way to visit family.

We were seated in a United Airlines 747 carrier heading for Chicago. We had been chatting about the weather, how it had been doing weird things globally, though "warming" was only one spooky possibility. There was a lull in the conversation when La pensively said, "You know what went through my mind before I opened my mouth at that party in Bel Air?" I shook my head in the negative though I knew exactly what party she was referring to. We had never spoken of that night and that particular party, which was not unusual for us. We had grown to accept life surrounding us as its own script writer. As far as possible we had also made a pact to fight against being judgmental about others, including ourselves. It was an on-going struggle, but we felt it a worthy practice. I already knew La had forgiven Missy. I felt it during the actual incident. That was another practice we worked at. We had figured out, as youngsters, that one: gossip was a mean way to exchange information; and two: being unforgiving was a sure way to make yourself sick. Our friendship went way beyond rehashing anything but the essence of before and only then if it connected to what was happening at the moment or to the path we had both chosen to walk: The path of love.

La went on, "I said a quick prayer. I asked God to be wholly with me." Well that certainly didn't surprise me. We both knew the power of prayer and used it regularly. We also regularly spoke about "God moments" in our lives. I said, "Your reply to Missy was certainly inspired. That's for sure."

La frowned. "Oh, that wasn't my God moment. I felt the *presence* and the *answer* to my prayer in the offing of Stick-Man's and Betty Oak's reactions. They were the "God moment" that rendered a very awkward incident undone!"

We were both quiet for a while. Then La spoke again, "You know, forgiveness is just about the sweetest, most potent medicine we have at our disposal. If we can just hold our peace when insulted or attacked and keep ourselves from reacting in kind, we can actually be the peacemakers we spiritually know we ought to be. I mean, what is the point of acting reactionary and getting bent out of shape over some slight or nasty business? None of us are at our best all the time. Sometimes we act out of the worse in ourselves."

I looked at my lifelong friend with new appreciation. We agreed that having being exposed to the spiritual workshops we attended, as regularly as we attended parties and church, had given us an edge that was invaluable. It was at one of those spiritual sessions that we learned about the power of mindfulness. Only someone who stayed in touch with mindfulness would be sharp enough to pray for guidance immediately after being insulted. Both of us thanked God again for having been under the guidance of Thich Nhat Hanh (his real name!) during one precious extended weekend retreat at a Buddhist monastery in the beautiful mountains of Southern California.

We spent the remaining time of our "plane trip" talking about how many different ways The Creator works through us and with us; how She protects and rescues us from the snare of the noisome pestilence on a moment to moment basis.

Our good talk reduced our journey in the sky to a super fast flight, much of it sprinkled with laughter, all the way to O'Hare airport and the city where "the hawk" and a great, Great Lake rules all life.

I'll end this tale by an addendum: Nothing that occurred at the party I've related here was ever mentioned in the press. It would have been juicy fodder for the rags, but it had been held in the palatial estate of a very powerful, *feared,* yet gracious man. Celebrities who are invited to his palatial estate know they are safe from the press without media *misinterpretation or exaggeration* of their behavior; that's why the man's festivities are always gladly attended. It was said that one time a reporter did crash one of his lavish affairs undetected. Following that party a scandalous story was printed about several guests and their wild doings there. That reporter not only lost his career, but the newspaper and the magazine that printed the story are now defunct! Anyway, there's no point in trying to figure out who is who, or who **was** what! I believe I've camouflaged all the who, what, and where's pretty good.

And who am I, you might ask? You can call me Onie.

QUIET FIRE

Rosa Parks parked herself on the front seat of a Jim Crow bus in 1955 Montgomery, Alabama, and busted all the prevailing godfathers of the day! But it wasn't that shy rose who did this deed in order to spark a Civil Rights Movement. That was not her intent. She was just a very tired sister wanting to rest from physical exertion as well as mental exertion brought on by extreme prejudice. There was a seat available on the bus and she took it. Through that simple gesture, she exerted her role as a daughter and disciple of the Rose of Sharon and made history.

It was God, with a big "Gee" who *used* the quiet vessel of this unsuspecting and private child. God plucked her out of Phoenix embers to light the fire of His collective suns, ripe and ready for a super nova rebirth. She was a reluctant heroine, much like her hero, Dr. Martin Luther King, Jr. He too, would not have picked himself for such a world altering role. But she accepted being "chosen" by being herself.

Mrs. Parks was one of the few persons you could *look* at and *know*—without a doubt—that she was not one for idle chatter. I could see it in photos of her and it was most revealing in television footage. But, many years ago I was privileged to meet her at the J.C. Bilbrew Library in Los Angeles, where she and Cab Calloway were being honored. I had been asked to write a poem for Mr. Calloway and Debbie Allen read my work. It was a wonderful night. However, the highlight for me was meeting Rosa Parks. I held her hand gently in both of mine, rather than shake it, when we were introduced. It seemed the most natural thing to do because, up close, she projected those "still waters" folk talk about. I didn't even try to ripple her humility with conversation. She murmured the softest greeting to me and her eyes sparkled with warmth. I felt revived. It was just "gooder" than good being in the same room with her. And I knew that, on this planet, Rosa Parks could truly be thought of as a "mouse that roared" or, even better, as a bus-people mountain mover!

D' DRUM

(Dedicated to My Brother, Stephen)

(Note: After the horrific kidnapping and enslaving of Africans, those who found them-
selves in North America were forbidden to make, use, or play any form of the drum. Those
Africans who wound up in South America or the Caribbean were "allowed" drumming—
after a struggle—and thus, stayed true to their innate rhythms. In the Caribbean, the Afri-
can need for the drum drove creativity to a new height and the "Steel Drum" was invented.
However, the U.S.A.'s "dum-dee-*drum*-dum" was a very different story and was the impetus
for a new music to come into being that would affect the whole world in a joyous high;
mainly in the mystical language of togetherness.)

In the cards of music

He was the king of sharps.

Miles ahead of us,

Inches behind his own angst.

Sparks sprinkled, bristled

Off his sound,

Shooting rainbows 'round my person,

Falling gently, skydiving thru

The fabric of my soul.

Transported by sound-waves,

Sounds from a music, a force

Greater than itself even unto this day,

I was shocked into completion.

I fell from my moorings into the

Abyss of Love

And found my true self rising

Out of star-cooled ash.

Burned beyond recognition I

Rise still in a Maya Angelou poem,

A balm soothing this self I am.

And now, married to the music, if not the muse,

I travel on high notes and low

Throaty trombone growls.

I bow to a bass being bowed by a master,

Wailing me to the depths of whale song.

I speed thru cosmos under the spell

Of pianos keyed into commission by the fingers

Of giants taking giant steps.

Jazz is a word, nothin' but a word of dubious origin

Just like the people from whom it springs.

"Nobody Knows My Name" James B. said one day,

And sho' he was right!

The music and the originators are yet unknowable;

Their reason for being a guessing game.

But being a force greater than itself, we grace this troubled orb

Half-conscious of the miracle,

Protected by a certain and sure enigma.

And I wondered at spelling out and spilling

The core of our mystique,

For truly this world is historically and spiritually

Unequipped to enjoy itself!

But faith brings with it a message so clear,

So profound, it trumpets a vision beyond

My kin or reality.

It shouts from Brownie's Cliff, high as Paradise:

"Earth is gonna make it, baby, cuz it's

The promised plan in Love's designated notes!"

And who am I to demur from so sacred a task?

It is a privilege and a joy to be transported by art,

Whether gifted or merely absorbed.

Thru art life is sanely revealed;

Becomes one and the same.

And one is the downbeat in

The Basie of all ac'Counts!

I have enjoyed a lifetime of music;

The inner-planes of its origins propelling me

On and on and way outside

For lo these many years.

I traverse far above the common ground.

There I live.

There I stay.

There I groove,

Yesterday, today, and all the tomorrows left

In my right mind rhythm.

AACM, holy hook-up, extending the song;

Recreating this jazz that only knows movement—

That has no standing still in it—

Not even in the underground of the wee-tall hours

To which it has been assigned, lest it wake the masses

And free us from mediocrity.

Yes! This so-called jazz is truly a key to that freedom we seek.

Call it "jazz" if you will

But know that it is sacred—

As holy as a church, whether you join it or not.

Our choices, rhythm-wise/church-wise, or otherwise, do not make God less real,

But being touched by our feelings has value sure as each note appeals to our souls delight.

Know that the Spirit Drum evoked jazz

And Be-Bop made it real:

Sealed it

And delivered it

By a swiftly soaring Yard Bird.

And that drum!?

That drum—

That Spirit Drum,

With no dead memories,

Gave eclectic juice to dem bones, dem bones, dem dry, dry bones.

That new drum beat me up and down

These roads less traveled;

These high ways of knowing this was no

Ordinary rhythm I was dancing and trancin' to!

Willed and willing to go with it,

It killed me.

I was gassed beyond possibilities,

And I died nine times life all at once.

Billy Higgins hugged us into communion.

Max Roach challenged our crawling and

We leapt to our feet.

Tony Williams confiscated our collective will and made us give it up.

Elvin Jones makes our free-fall effortless.

Art Blakeley arrested us in mid-flight and injected us with fearlessness.

Steve McCall made us weep with joy.

Idris Muhammad familiarized us

With the oases within

And we followed him to the desert.

We camel-walked all the way back to our president,

Lester Young, who was living on Billie's

Strange Fruit.

Pres poured sweet water for us to drink

As we blinked in the blinding light left by

The cosmic trails of Satchmo and Ledbetter.

Then we knew—

We knew better!

The drum had been returned in a newborn code

Fit only for the progeny of former slaves whose spirits

Were being tested, sometimes bested, often

Wresting formidable odds into incredible genius.

A new drum to be beaten by a new people nearly beaten to death.

A brand new drum struck with a brand new beat to be replete until the planet grows

"Cool."

Know that the new music is stronger than all its broken parts put together.

Know that it lives as long as forever exists.

Know that Sun Ra gave us secrets for free—

With glee, of the galaxies.

He couldn't help it, being the son of radical rays

From a smoking gun,

His finger ever on the trigger of his Arkestra-ship.

That wasn't no train on plain tracks

I made my passage on!

My ticket got stamped at the Savoy and

The Trianon on my way to a

Limitless destiny.

I'm riding the 'Trane where brains get changed

At stations of total awareness.

The fare is fair and

Only depends on how wide I open whatever

I am willing to share.

It doesn't matter whose song you choose to ride your way to consciousness

Or where you play with your jazzy self.

Know that you are safe on John's Trane,

In Abbey's Lincoln,

On the elegant Ellington Express,

On Horace's Silver Bullet,

And certainly in Monk's Time Ma-Swing!

Know that jazz is being struck alive somewhere

On this planet at all times, its vibes secure

In the capable "Bags" of Milt Jackson;

Grooving, with all your necessary stuff

Packed in tenderness.

Know that your final destination is not

A termination, but an arrival

To the best there is in yourself.

Know that jazz is a sacred

weapon of mass salvation

Come to Earth to heal, but first the music *has to* "Kill" ya!

Early jazz albums were recorded to **drop balms on us!**

So--listen to some jazz "killers" often and get well soon.

A SUPER-CONSCIOUS PRAYER

I pray for the Nazi's, the "Skin-Heads", the haters in general, the Klansmen and the Klanswomen. I pray for the hostile and the angry, the jealous and the greedy, the war-mongers, and gang-bangers.

My heart goes out to the guilty and the innocent alike.

I pray that lost souls be found by God's mightiest agents, that healing angels touch their hearts at the core with love.

A special prayer for those called "Illuminati" (or other self-serving titles). May the heavenly heart surgeon of compassion slash through their self-importance and illuminate their souls with new depths of caring for others.

I pray that all Earth's enemies be made tranquil and void of all their negativity.

I pray that the evil lurking and abiding in their souls be laid so low as to disappear into the thinnest air.

I pray for love to be seeded, right now, in all those who would do harm to themselves and to others. I pray for love seeds to grow like wild fire in their hearts, their minds, and their spirits.

Let love slip into all the cracks and crannies of their sleep and cast a new itch upon them that they **must,** *indeed,* scratch or go completely mad from unexpressed joy! In Jesus' name I pray. Selah.

FEARLESS

The fact that we created "Kings" and invented "governments"

proves that our formal history was born in self-doubt and self-loathing.

Thus, "everyday people" re-created hell on Earth

and have been living it ever since.

It should be no wonder then,

or come as no surprise,

that peasants grovel and slaves rebel,

certain to rise after a spell.

But the wisest king always knows,

without being told,

he is just a regular Joe

with a mojo on him.

And my advice to those,

faint of heart, yet

striving to be human and humane

even in the face of so much evidence

indicating profit otherwise:

Don't give up so soon!

Be fearless!

Choose Love

every day.

Don't be sore.

Soar!

A LOOK AT US
FROM THE UNIVERSAL SPACE STATION

Out here, far above our planet, we are a beautiful sight. The Earth is revealed as a huge blue-white marbled globe spinning on an expanse of black velvet space of inestimable depth. Only a few man-made objects can be discerned from way up here on the face of the Earth, but not a human being is in sight. Looking at Earth from MIR, mankind is merely non-existent!

Those who got the privilege of traveling to outer-space – those who take the incredible photos of our heavenly home for us to see – are given many gifts to treasure for the rest of their lives. Two of those gifts are renewed awe and deep humility. Astronauts and cosmonauts are never quite the same after returning to Earth after being in outer-space. Their scientific minds can never put into words of true comprehension what they have experienced because their hearts, their feelings become overwhelmingly involved. They then evolve to a new human level of consciousness. But one thing is abundantly clear: They, as well as those of us who will never experience an astronomical journey, have been touched profoundly in the *same exact* way by the revelation of the Earth photo-shoot! We have all been "quickened" – further awakened – in our hearts.

Seeing ourselves from the perspective of the space station has given us a rare, perhaps first-time super-nova heart-mind collaboration on a collective basis.

We humans have a history of fighting against our hearts being pierced except by Cupid's arrow or by familial closeness. Otherwise we are more intellect driven, which is sad since it is our heart's development that is at the core of our Earthly salvation.

Perhaps, then, the new revelations from seeing Earth on the deeps is the most *important* reason for the success of the space program. In the spiritual evolution of our collective understanding of life, I know this to be the truth.

From the cosmic point of view we can be thought of as seven billion microscopic organisms inhabiting an orbiting blue island out here in a galaxy of hope and hopelessness. Indeed, our home planet is miniscule in the Universal schematic which reduces humanity even less than microscopic!

That being said, human beings can also be looked at in several ways in terms of their importance as passengers aboard the Earth-ship sailing in the Milky Way Galaxy. We are, in a sense, biological parasites plundering our host-mother of her many endowments, both for sustenance and profit. We can also, just as truthfully, be seen as caretakers of Earth, using its treasures for elevated invention, pleasure, and a kind of spiritual root-base for our collective evolution.

However, viewed in terms of our generations on Earth, we have come to a point in our development where self-destruction looms (seemingly) larger than any other evolutionary collective consciousness. That is why an ancient idea with a fresh approach to continue life is imperative in order to survive, and then hopefully *thrive* as a force yet unsung throughout the Milky Way and beyond.

We are being pulled in opposite directions, waging a tug-of-war with one another. One pole sees, rightly, a need for saving our planet and its inhabitants from further abuse and obvious total devastation by reducing, or eliminating, our greed and the continuous misuse of our planet's gifts. Though the other pole supporters have energy to burn, they are spiritual arsonists. They subvert knowledge, impede unity, and torch meaningful togetherness on the whole with divisionism.

A tiny percentage of Earth's human family controls the production and wealth of resources available from this planet. These self-important persons harvest, reap, and sell both the necessities and especially the wants of all the other "family" members who are not so blessed with ways and means of enhancing their own development without this dependence. Rarely acknowledged however, but astonishingly true, all dependencies have sponsors of equal dependence! Of course we are talking about, and looking at, material gain and convenience as well as man's need for daily sustenance. This is only partially true since all persons have been blessed with some measure of independence in supplying their own needs—whether they accept this given or not. It is a dichotomy begging to be solved that keeps the masses dependent on the few.

We are said to be different from our other biological, botanical, and zoological companions because we *think* and we *reason*. Ah yes, we humans have thoughts and ideas of lofty invention as well as banal repetition. We certainly do use brain power to consider all sorts of things. We have erected monuments that inspire and have created great dams that hold back rivers. We have sent skyscrapers high against the heavens, made airplanes that transport us all around the globe. We have made all kinds of technological and communicative inventions that link us to each other across the whole world. We have made space stations with telescopes that penetrate other galaxies beyond our own. But rarely do we contemplate, think-before-we-speak, lift love above all else in true realism, or use our gifts of imagination beyond the romantic, the coming together through natural or unnatural disaster, or taking sides in the theatrical aisles of war. We have all but forgotten how to dream. We'd rather follow the leader. We'd rather scheme.

We are dearly wonderful souls or can be the worse for wearing out our welcome. At any given moment we are everything in between wonderful and absolutely awful. Most of us are combinations of varying extremes. This, because we have the mysterious and marvelous gift of choice on a personal level while (at the same time) we are all subjects of the rulings of weather, planetary changes, serendipity, and other phenomena that render us totally helpless without much choice at all. Think of droughts, disease, tornadoes, tsunamis, sinkholes, volcanoes (on the brink of eruption), wars that disrupt our lives without our permission, that car you didn't see coming, crashing commodity markets, and crop circles!

We are creations formed by the omnipotent mystery of God; created for God's pleasure, I hear, and I can hardly divine what else could have been in God's mind when creating us! This understanding has a powerful impetus on the heart and mind of the believer. It lifts us out of cosmic insignificance to heavenly assignation. I doubt that God needed "reason", as we define it, to create us, for reason is the potent potion of our fumbling logic!

All I know for certain is that God is not part of the logical wonders of this life because GOD IS LOVE! And with that succinct definition we can safely say that love, the way we reckon it, is absolutely out of the neat realm of logic. Of course the heart resonates with truth and has its own logistical reasoning at work all the time.

Most of us are only lovable on occasion anyway. Thank God our being lovable is not a necessary prerequisite for being loved! Mostly we are self-indulgent creatures of worry and folly and hesitation marked by blind foolishness. We constantly devalue love and we gravitate toward gaining more money. Some say that, "love makes the world go 'round", while others are convinced that money controls practically every aspect of life.

We know that this planet is spinning around on its axis out here in space. Perhaps we should be "spinning" more love in our Earth's orbit rather than concentrating on spending money! It's a thought.

Now, money is very, very important to us until we recognize how little money and material wealth is truly meaningful or capable of making us happy. And since happiness is our most manifest goal, it is amazing that an alarming number of us cast our lots in the money game way before we even give love or happiness a second thought. We scramble around in a frenzy of activity to accumulate money and to get more "stuff." We gamble our youth in this way until we either "wake up" or become aged, sick in body, mind, and/or spirit. Only then do we appear to realize how little money and things have to do with being honestly alive. Then we would trade all the money we possess if only our physical bodies would miraculously heal to peak condition. We would give up all of our material goods for perfect health, either for ourselves or for a loved one, and take our chances in a world that is not only bent on making us like everybody else (thus rendering us obedient slaves to the status quo), it intentionally robs us of our unique individuality. This world, as we have disorganized it, would have us groveling in poverty both physically and spiritually, but sharing the wealth means more than distributing money fairly. "Sharing the wealth" has much more to do with expressing and activating compassion, good will, and peace more than other things. That is why we make saints out of those who make a practice of being kind and giving beyond the norm. In actuality, it should be "normal" to be kind and generous.

Just as every grain of sand is unique, we too have the spark of specialness in our make-up, but the sand becomes a beach or establishes itself as "baby-mountains" of great dunes. The sands do this through *togetherness*! That is what is missing from our supreme evolution.

Let it be known that "sharing the wealth" will not cure aging or certain death, but it is the panacea of true *brotherhood* (even writing that word—*brotherhood*—makes me feel almost sophomoric and silly, so inured to togetherness has our planetary psyche become!), and an easement of poverty of the spirit, the physical body, and the mental anguish that assails so much of humanity. Is that a responsibility that we have missed? Yes! Because no matter how we slice up the pie that charts our course on Earth, we are ONE people and ONE family of a specified order—gifted or doomed to a collective fate—depending on the majority point of reference coupled with positive action or total devastation awaiting us (unless we are blessed with a miracle come to rescue us from ourselves—again, but I have a nagging suspicion that we have misused most of the miracles granted us in the past as well as daily miracles we constantly miss or dismiss)! Sharing the wealth is so much more than easements through the fair distribution of money. (That ain't gonna happen on this planet. I am not that naïve nor blinded by that notion, and besides, some of us are going to be severely shocked when money all over the world becomes totally worthless! Don't be surprised.) True sharing brings with it riches beyond the snare of money or the accumulation of things. It encompasses sharing the love, sharing the respect, sharing smiles, sharing grace, and sharing pieces of the puzzle of life with one another. The more we do these things, the more answers unfold themselves before us, almost like magic. It is part of universal law: When we give the best of ourselves to one another, we are graced by even deeper understandings of the mysteries of life.

With all our ills, woes, and often disgusting acts of things like hate, violence, and utter apathy, there are those who are cognizant of true values and riches. They are more than compensated for their short sojourns here because they keep their feet firmly planted under the table that hosts the extraordinary feast that is life for the taking and making. The best things in life are not only free, but are unconditional in their scope and depth. I think of the great film, "Doctor Zhivago" and the scene that burned its lesson in my heart. It happened when the Russian elite and the rebellious against the prevailing regime are arrested and thrown together in trains for deportation away from all that they have known. Only one man railed against the injustice of it all and would not allow himself to be made into the new regimes' definition of who he was and how he was supposed to behave. And it occurred to me that he was the only one "free" in that railroad car which is why he was the only one handcuffed! All the other "prisoners" strained to find some normalcy in their situation, but their stress was so vivid it became a living presence running through each and every one of them. They were pressed together like sardines, but they were obedient in their defeat. Not so, with the handcuffed man: He had the untamed fire of life coursing through him and he inspired Dr. Zhivago in the movie, and me transported to higher realms from my seat in a darkened theater.

One love around the Earth, upon the Earth, within the Earth, by the people, for the people, through the birth of higher consciousness of the people today…tomorrow…and on into perpetuity!

What a fabulous idea!

Well, that's my warm, fuzzy dream. I know there are hundreds, if not millions, of folk who would simply gag in competitive annoyance over such a notion! They are the regulated regulators of the forces of currency, dividing and presumably, keeping the rest of us controlled and conquered. They are unmoved by the currents of peace and harmony and love. They don't mind war at all. Some even love it. They are pimples on the ass of progress! To suggest that peace is unequivocally necessary for the revival of a planet in desperate need of survival would only evoke a bored yawn from the less evolved souls among us. Do not be fooled! These apathetic souls and/or detractors of progress only appear to be the majority as projected by an international media controlled by big business and bent on keeping us obedient to minority rule even while they screw us royally! Know that the overwhelming majority of humans are decent, life-loving souls who live by random acts of kindness every single minute.

More and more evolved human beings are finding one another and sharing the healing, spiritual energy, and loving intellect of this growing age of collective evolution. The energy is seeping into every facet of our lives and is remaining independent of the status quo. It is a quiet thing, for the most part, but it has such formidable power it breaks through the barriers of media spins, political biases, and other old, tried and brewed methods reserved for frightening the wits out of the masses in order to maintain the existing state of affairs!

We are at the brink of positive breakthrough and that is why it seems so dire and difficult. The moment of immediate birth is always critical. We must not give up hope or allow "bad news" to throw us off the path. We must stay centered, stay positive, choose to be happy every day, and decide upon arising to be—just for today—the highest being of ourselves. Once we make these choices habit, we find ourselves gifted in so many ways, I dare not enumerate lest you look for my miracles to happen in your life and thus, miss your own!

I feel such a quiet joy even knowing what I do about myself, my species, and the world around me. I have a couple of certainties that fuel my passion and my dreams. One concerns the essence of peace, its healing and its power.

Peace is a monumental drive of such magnitude that it has no need to **force** itself on the unwilling. Peace is the mainframe of understanding and health. Peace is never distant from us. We are born with it in tow as part of our spiritual DNA (Divine Natural Attributes). It is ever with us, except we constantly disturb it in ourselves and in our relationships. This is so because we have been taught **fear** and have become paralyzed by that ugly phenomenon. Worse than that, but oh so subtly connected, is the non-rational source of apathy that surrendering to fear creates in the masses. But, praise God, peace always wins the day even if it has to wait for one's last breath. Peace is patience personified.

It is said that every grain of sand and every single snowflake is unique; no two are exactly alike. I liken myself to the Saharan desert and the North Pole. I wrap their amazing existence around my oneness with them, my frame of reference, and with all that is. I feel microscopic and yet, as big as the entire universe.

I know that God cares for each and every one of us "snowflakes" on an individual basis even as we sleep (both with our eyes opened or closed!), but too many of us think so little of ourselves we melt into a smallness that freezes our gifts into unwrapped presence! I think it must insult every atom of our being and true calling.

I add my God-given power as an atomic balm to all life on Earth. I champion all those who reject the tired nightmare that would keep us asleep.

And

If I should wake before

I die,

I pray my soul expose

The lie

That keeps us from the greater love

And

Self-discovery.

UMPH!

Some say we were set up by

Humpty Dumpty--

that we've been doing the decline and

fall

of our own undoing since

that nursey rhyme

caught our collective timing.

A time when we began to forget about

natural rhythm and we

began the Beguine.

A time when we got in line

and on-line became as natural as queues and quotes.

A one-time-thing—yet—reminiscent of

Ancient Rome,

Zulu lulu's,

de Ja vu,

and other quests that

that keep us guessing.

We march to a media blitz magnet

with nary a thought

'cause we're having a ball

just by being

right on time

to a party line!

But blessed be the abiding one whose own drummer

is in concert with cosmic stuff.

Blessings galore

to

those who opt **not** to take the fall at all.

May you rise often

and then, may you

soar

the rest of the way **over** the long haul a comin' this fall.

WAKE UP, BROTHERS AND SISTERS, WAKE UP!

We've been urged to believe that war is something that resorts from some kind of "necessary evil." I have to question the necessity of war as a means to solve anything, but I definitely agree that war is evil personified. However, I also agree that at this time in our march toward true civilization, we must have armed forces to protect our so-called boundaries from invasion. But "protection" and "invasion" are very different aspects that might (or might not) require an armed solution. And the "boundaries" that we so jealously guard, like puffed up roosters, should not be lines drawn on the earth to keep us apart.

The thing about war is that it is the most obscene preoccupation of man on planet Earth.

Conversely, copulation is made to be unseemly for the young and an eternal battle for self-control among the mature.

Sex-laden movies are rated X and such, but the bestial calamity that is war has become mother's milk for our young. We even buy our children toy guns to "play" with!

It is a good thing when children witness their parents being affectionate with one another and sharing good-will with others outside the home. Psychiatry, psychology, theology, physiology, and all the other isms and "…ologies" agree that affection and good-will are wholesome and nourishing, generating health by exposure.

The worse pornography ever filmed at its lousiest is Michealangelo in motion and Romare Beardon in purity compared to the still-life death objective of war. War is active treason to civilization, peace, well-being, truth, and progress.

The delineation of power is at the root of war for whatever disagreement one country has with another or between two people whose relationship begins to disintegrate. But anger and weapons of destruction are not the answer to solve personal or global disagreements.

There are no disagreements that cannot be ameliorated by respectful intellectual intercourse. If we are willing to spend decades fighting and killing one another over oil rights and weapons of mass destruction, surely we can send our brightest and wisest to the round table of satisfaction no matter how long it takes! We waste the little brain matter awakened in us to do otherwise. Until we learn to use our minds for discourse to solve our differences on the national, as well as, in the international arena we will continue to hurl, like mad comets, toward collective insanity instead of collective evolution.

Whatever your beliefs, dogma, karma, grudges, or grief, use your energy to heal our troubled world. Become an atomic balm bearing soothing medicine emanating from your heart, your mind, and your spirit.

I happen to be a Christian soldier by "draft" and design, but **together**, you and I, no matter our religious or other "differences" become the power of love as **weapons of mass salvation.** Let us meet in respect and gratitude for the gift of our lives. Let us reason with one another beyond the barriers that would keep us apart. Let us tear down the walls of separation that would keep us in fear and disgust.

I do not look like you. I do not worship as you do. I do not dress like you. I have my ways and you have yours. We are only as different as we deem is so. I cry the same as you. I laugh and so do you. I grieve sometimes as do you. All our vowels have the same meaning even though our native languages are different, but with so many differences, I can still say with all my heart that I love you just as you are. I honor your right to be you. I pray for your well-being, for your success, and for your children to grow strong and happy. When I celebrate life, I am also celebrating you as part of my Earth family. Do NOT be afraid of me, for I am your own sister and your mirror out here breathing free and reflecting harmony. Be at peace knowing that I am here in these yet-to-be-*United*-States, and no matter where you are, you are part of my prayer for a true and lasting peace.

THE DUKE OF ELLINGTON

Long before Eldridge called us "Queens..."

Way before he made my sisters come in droves

as he strove through his painful reconciliation

with himself, and

decades before the beautiful Cleaver

slashed away the persistent lie

that sullied black womanhood...

another man made love to us

in such a way

time cannot forget

and

history cannot erase.

Royal in every sense of the word,

this master, who ruled the dukedom of music

rhapsodized our stolen beauty.

He honeycombed our straightening irons

and neutralized our skin lighteners

"In a Mellow Tone."

And we quietly,

in the still of our plight,

took flight on the piercing vehicle of his song.

I was unaware,

on "The A-Train,"

wearing a cheap dress under duress

when he addressed me

as "The Brown-skinned Girl in the Calico Dress."

And suddenly

I sat up

dressed up!

Then,

Just about the time

when I was blooming into what I did not know,

it was Duke who showed me

I was a "Passion Flower."

(My petals continue to unfold

since that bold awakening!)

I became a "Satin Doll";

a dream girl in a "Black and Tan Fantasy."

I eased into a "Sophisticated Lady"

was part of the "High Life."

One day a "Creole Love Song"

drifted in my open window

and I crystallized into a "Black Butterfly".

Years later a white composer

paid tribute to black femininity.

He penned a pretty tune and called it,

"Georgia Rose, Georgia Rose."

Tony Bennett chose to give it life.

I dig Tony Bennett:

His dignity, his humanity, his politics, and his licks.

But as pretty as that song is,

a wrong message

gets stuck in the needle

of my groove…with those lyrics,

"Don't be blue 'cause you're black, Georgia Rose, Georgia Rose…"

Say whaaaat!?

I ain't nevah been blue 'cause I'm black!

But being human

I have definitely had the blues!

So let us set "the blues" in whole notes:

I got uptight from a long conglomeration of chains

skillfully linked to keep us down:

Lack of this, lack of that,

"Bell Curves" thrown at us,

tossed from unbalanced scales

without a do re mi on either end;

closed doors and back seats,

out and out lies spread on you

like flies on bread oozing faux butter,

and having your laughter stolen from you

just because you were born with it!

It was us looking at our babies,

looking back at us

with that mother/child double question mark,

a stark and painful stare:

Should I share the stain for future fare

to pay and gain so little?

The blues is watching our talents rise,

ablaze in the sky,

only to tumble like falling stars

while a meager few make a place for themselves

permanently…

oh yeah, and without royalties

'cause loyalty left with theft!

It's watching our men strive to thrive

on rejection

and failing that,

reject us for the mirror we cannot help but reflect.

Oh Yes!

The blues for black women,

more often than not,

is the black man!

But with the help of Billie Holiday, Dinah Washington, Big Maybelle

Lena, Ella and Aretha,

we put a whippin' on those blues so 'tuff

we often extract Duke's "Blues Indigo!".

Sho' nuff!

Just about the time when the world

turned upside down…

when the new messenger was struck down…

when my mind became a frown…

when my brothers,

dashiki's on their backs,

the latest Playboy magazine between their legs,

the status-quo wrapped around their brains,

us in their hearts—

and me—moaning,

sitting around with my chin in my hand—

"Here we go 'round the old cycle again!"

Just at that moment,

my memory band did me

a sweet, sweet favor.

And I heard

the super-slick, deep soul voice of

Edward Kennedy Ellington

whisper in my ear,

"ZZaj, darling, a drum is a woman!

A drummmm is a WOE-MAN!"

Well,

beat me daddy, eight to the bar!

I got on up and

off the cycle trick:

I left the revolution of the phonograph record,

The revolution of the revolving door of persecution,

the so-called "grounded revolution"

and got ready for the further evolution of me!

Duke sure can help a sister get her hand back on her hip

when she gets hip enough!

(Happy Birthday Duke, April 29, 1975)

A VERY RUDE AWAKENING

BEFORE I MET YOU I DIDN'T EVEN KNOW I HAD SKIN!

DUST FROM THE DREAM

Rhetoric solving clichés

Resound thru the masses.

Truths,

Like man's inhumanity to man

Surface.

Alarm bells toll…

Grave.

Grave.

Depending on one's company

All agree with

The proper solution:

Love

Or

Wither in the freezing chill of

Indifference.

And the cry

Ebbs and flows

Thru the massive sea

Of fearful folk.

What's to be done

Sighs concerned…

Start with self

Returns enlightened…

Is it too late

Trembles sad…

Perhaps for America

Chimes the bruised citizen.

And all the time

Nature edges herself

Farther away from

The safety valve

As she unleashes the terrifying results

That presses her watch.

Earth is helpless before

Her duty;

Her cosmic design to

Protect and heal thru Love,

To break and destroy

From indifference.

She can only respond in kind

To God's own law.

II.

Would that trees or

Bees or baboons or berries

Been given dominion over Earth!?

Anything…!

To direct this force in the turning now

Toward a decent dimension.

Then an orderliness might prevail

With the seasons.

Man would copulate and populate

According to his tender time;

Would tell the hour

By his feelings;

Would value cultivation and his children;

Would hunt for warmth and closeness

And eat according to his teeth and

Digestion;

Would marvel over the miracle

In quietude;

Would grow in caring calculation

Of his existence

In the natural schematic;

Would laugh at the antics

Of his own provoked wonder;

Would not be afraid of death;

Would compose wood and sand,

Fire and water

Into musical canvases;

Would art his mathematics into

Soluble atoms

That dance for daylight;

Would brighten his corner of the universe into

A vastness worthy of heavens own

Expansion;

Would rise and rise above

The meanness of his span

And link with eternity in the master plan;

Would sing cotton into cloth;

Would witness

The silk worm roll in the mud ball's turning

Of sublime surrender;

Would witness

The lamb shed its wool for the needy stock;

Everything green and fruitful

Would bestow its best;

Would witness

His intelligence evolve with ease and

Thanksgiving.

And man would partake unto

His share and delight.

He would learn from the star.

He would lend upon need.

He would lean upon proof.

He would not limp, no leech, nor lie, nor lynch, nor leer, nor lust, nor

Limit his brother's unfolding.

He would laugh!

He would leap across lechery!

He would lift and

He would light into

Awakening 'til

He could rule himself in Love.

III.

But,

We have not reached that

Kindergarten in the

Garden.

We are still despoiled of

Our own unmaking

While we marvel at our

Mirror which is

Cracked in the camera's lie.

We shoot pictures

And each other.

We mean well and pollute wells

In the meanwhile.

We make enemies of our selves

As we double dare death with drugs

We go thru the day

Begging for cash anesthetics

And just a few more toys.

We settle for less and less until

Our best is so tarnished,

We second our used-to-be's

Into first class sales for

The next generation.

We fool around with transference

And transcendence.

We transport time to a despicable destination.

We even ransom music

And kill its true melody:

O, don't you know

You are being beaten

To death

For real by a

Beat

That did not come from

Musicians

But from

Beaten composers

Broken by a

Beast

That is grateful to be dead!?

That is not music that you snake to

But the amused-Mint

Mutilating your minds!

We compute our weather into

Whether we like it or not,

And chase the cloud we made

That kills.

Yet, every once in a great shocked while

We stop.

We stop on the warped beat

Of our weak descending.

We stop just long enough to

Repeat

Our mother's mistakes

And draw upon her

Wisdom

Only when we wonder

Why the United States

Are not

United!?

Then all the reason she wore herself

Out trying to teach us

Comes to fore and

We know…

At last we understand

That we, as a species,

Are enthralled with murder

And thoroughly ashamed of

Love.

So,

Earth, (you) have no choice.

I do not blame you.

I do not quake

Before your fury.

Go on now,

Do your utmost to render us

Paid in full

For our sleep-walking-foolishness.

We deserve your poisoned innocence

And your cosmic wrath.

But, I do weep.

I confess I sigh.

I do bow in reverence

Beneath each blow,

Each glancing lie.

I do shrink with each disaster

Called "natural;"

For I miss the brothers and sisters

That I will never meet

(not even in the whispered unison of prayer and atmospheric breath)

I do sigh

Because it could be

Lovely.

I do sigh, in the deeply bedded marrow

Of my sorrow,

Because it should be

Beautiful.

FOR EVERYBODY

In the final analysis

All we've got is God.

There is really nothing else.

God is the cake of life.

And me—

And my next breath,

Plus you,

Are the icing

Clinging to the Cake

In praise

And gratefulness.

THE HAIKU DAYS OF SEPTEMBER

September 1

RIGHT HERE FROM MY ROOM

MIRACLES OF MIRACLES

I DO REACH

THE STARS!

September 2

A SPLINTER CAUGHT HER

AS SHE WORKED THE WOULD OF LIFE

AND IT CHANGED HER MIND.

September 3

(Clare and David)

PEACE, LIKE A RIVER,

SOOTHED THE WEARY TRAVELER

'TIL HE CAUGHT THE BOAT!

September 4

A BEGGAR GAVE UP

A BORROWER PLANNED HIS TAKE

A GIVER REACHED OUT.

September 5

IT IS NOT NEW NEWS

WHEN BLACK BOYS WIN THE BIG RACE—

IT'S A LIGHT STORY.

September 6

(Grandmother Lettie McCall)

MY CAT WAITS FOR ME

EVERY DAY AT SIX O'CLOCK

HE'S GOT MY NUMBER.

September 7

ROSE LEAVES, HIPS AND YOU--

WONDERMENT OF PAUSE AND CURE

STEEPED IN CHICAGO.

September 8

THE TELEPHONE RINGS,

SOMEONE IS IN NEED OF TOUCH;

THE EAR SUBSTITUTES.

September 9

ALWAYS LEND A HAND

WHENEVER THE NEED IS NIGH;

IT WILL BEST YOUR QUEST.

September 10

(Freddie)

A SPLENDID DAY

WITH ME AWARE OF THE STARS;

SUCH BALANCE MATTERS.

September 11

GOD ALONE KNOWS WHY--

YOU AND I CAN ONLY MUSE

OR SEEK SURRENDER.

September 12

SOME KNOW EVERYTHING—

LIKE DOPE IS THE WORST THERE IS!

OTHERS WATCH TV.

September 13

WILL WE EVER LEARN?

COMMERCIALS LEAD US ASTRAY.

IT'S NOT ABOUT HAIR!

September 14

(Anna J. Hicks)

RIDE THE BLACK STALLION;

THRUSTING HOOVES, SOFT SOD AND BREEZE—

THE WORLD PASSES BY.

September 15

SWEET MUSIC OF NOW,

PHRASED SURPRISE BEARING NEW HEIGHTS—

JAZZ OF PEACE AND LIGHT.

September 16

NO ONE MENTIONS THIS:

JAZZ IS THE MIRACLE KEY.

THAT IS WHY IT IS SUPRESSED!

September 17

AMERICA NAPS;

KEEPS THE MASSES IGNORANT.

THE GOVERNED-MINT RULES!

September 18

TEND THE GARDEN WELL.

THERE IS JAZZ AMONG THE PLANTS.

DON'T LOSE THE HARVEST.

September 19

THE EARTH AND I HURT.

GOD SAID SHE WOULD HEAL THE LAND.

SWEET JESUS, COME BACK!

September 20

IN THE SPOILS OF SPLICE,

OF MIX AND OVERDUBBING,

TRY TO SAVE THE SONG.

September 21

(Savannah)

REMOVE THE DESPAIR—

THE SOUL NEEDS COSMIC PLEASURE…

LOVE IS ON THE RISE!

September 22

THE WIND THRILLS MY BREATH—

IT SWEEPS THE WORLD IN SONG LIKE

A CAPPELLA LIFE!

September 23

YOU ARE THE CHANGE KEY—

THE CHALLENGE IS IN THE LOCK—

OPEN UP, BE FREE!

September 24

(Brandon)

CHICAGO, MY LOVE,

HOW YOU GROW AND STAY ALIVE

IS A MIRACLE!

September 25

BEING YOUR OWN BOSS

IS A MATTER OF WEATHER

WHEN YOU TEND THE LAND.

September 26

MY SOUL RULES FREELY

MY MIND IS A PLANE JUMPER

MY HEART LIVES IN LOVE.

September 27

PRAY FOR RAIN WITH ME—

MY AFRICA NEEDS CLOUD BREAKS.

WHET YOUR PRAYER WITH LOVE.

September 28

NOTHING HEALS LIKE TRUTH,

LIKE MED'CINE, TRUTH SOMETIMES HURTS;

LIKE WISDOM, TRUTH CURES.

September 29

LEAVES HAVE DYED THEIR CLOTHES.

NOW THEIR COLORS DANCE WITH WINDS!

SOON THE LEAVES WILL FLY.

September 30

(Stephen IV)

LOVE IS LIKE A BALM—

IT SOOTHES, IT SMOOTHES, IT SPREADS;

RUB ME DOWN WITH LOVE.

(Before an Atomic Balm Fell on me, I mostly cried…)

SOWETO

I remember the day Arthur Jenkins

Gave up…

Was the day of the beast

He said…

Six, sixteen, seventy-six,

700 black children lay wounded

Or dead.

School children,

Like ours,

Babies unarmed,

Killed by the agent of Satan--

And Arthur Jenkins

Repeated it over again…

All down the block

He tread.

He said

A sign from the Bible had come to

The fore

So he gave up his prayer and 4-squared;

Started living the word with

His life,

His own life;

He preaches on corners now

And then—

Can light up an el on a curve in the loop;

With a

6, 6, and 6 again:

He teaches us the number

And don't it make you wonder,

Why the *sign?*

Dig the crime!

Then it came—

Just like that!

6-16-76,

And South African children

Had

Paid the

Price

To save the world

Again!

Satan, walking thru

Apart-hate,

Only wanted the innocent

For his bait!

That's

Why the *sign*

For his crime

Against life

Against you

Against me.

And we let it happen—

Lots of good people

Forgetting to be human

Except for a whale or two;

A pat on the back

Or a TV rescue—

Just in time

With the *sign*

On prime time

And uh,

Six-Sixteen-Seventy-six…

The rumble was deep and

A whole heap keep lying

'bout the innocent,

The weak.

And the Earth stretches meek,

In harmony with the universe,

Trying to balance her life

In time

With other signs.

6—6—and 6 again…

And don't it make you wonder,

Why *that sign!*

Don't you see the crime and the slime who did it!?

But in the twinkling of St. Nick, we forget.

WAIL SONG

Whence-so-ever those big black holes that eat up light and show up the night?

How came they to be?

Was it from two old words so sincerely spoke they plunged on strokes that tore the sky asunder?

It makes me wonder!

Those two plain words that echoed thru a billion selves

Are painful swords

Striking the question off the shelves.

And the answer sweating on the speed of light, that booster fuel propelling Sight

So you and I can see,

A black whole filled completely…

A black bottom set free to dance without the stop-portunity.

Those two old words tow the past on a comet trail dragging fast the first

Somewhere in its tale.

And the black hole sighs,

In need of emptiness and release from all those whys.

I know an answer there does wait, but on the path I hesitate…

Two words so strong

They make me quake

Like the tremor in a song.

But on I go to Africa and there in the midst of a man-made drought I weep

As I watch a baby's bout

With body bloat and hunger's goad

Too weak to wave away the load

Or fend himself from the flies that extract the last moisture from its eyes.

As his mother lifts a weary arm to turn away the probing linger I drop my

Head, but catch the dust

Drifting, sifting off her fingers.

Crossing the continent to the North, I behold the wreck of Tripoli and check

The masses fleeing fate from one man's ego tripping sate…

From another man's slipping power date who dared to say no

To the other man's face!

Then I race away to the South and there I lose the breath from mouth for

Gaping right before all else is hell and fury and the fiend

Riding mean on casket rows…

Judge and jury blow on blows.

Deep in blood I swim that ocean heading West, past the isles

Trapped in the keep

Of America gone mad from cash on hand.

And there I'm met by a band of Navajos being further swept off their own land.

Filled with a growing ghetto dread I

Cower from the PCP as it spreads like poison on my bread,

Plus slaps me right up side my head!

The stars I see fly me out in space where I am drawn toward the hole…

That hole caused by those cold words:

Unanswered script rent to quasar rift that pulls me to a nightmare's drift…

My tears cry No!

I reject all flight as the words rush toward my desperate plight.

They reach my side, sear like a spear, rip thru my chest,

Burning straight for my throat and I scream out of me all the way to the

Pitch that lightens up the dark:

How lonnnng!

THE REAL STATUS OF LIBERTY

Ms Liberty was scaffold in a cage

For months

And that's when I felt her;

That's when she meant something to me.

Except for the reasons behind her apparent

Captivity

We could have come to this shore

Together

(bound and trussed up by an untrustworthy foible).

For months I haunted the harbor

Gazing on the steady hand of liberty behind bars,

Her torch as black as my night and her

Face streaked with dirt.

She looked tired, tried, judged, exhausted and caught.

100 years of bringing in the wolves dressed

Like raggedy sheep

Who would hardly wait for the salt water to dry

Before they addressed me in hate.

She looked wasted,

Ms. Liberty did.

A modern day Noah, she had invited groups,

Not two by twos

Of runaways, escape artists, down 'n outs, cons

And protagonists of tag.

And they came in droves

From all over Europa

They came.

And then they became persecutionists

Of the first order...

They did.

Escaping the pain of their own birth wrongs

They came.

They were humbled by the sight of Lady Liberty herself,

And they wept real tears and hugged their young'uns close;

Held each other up to the vision

Towering over the harbor

Like a saint dropped down from

Heaven itself.

They didn't look for no Native Americans,

However,

Would have dropped dead if they'd seen one,

But they sure did look for me.

They knew I was here before any one of them

And they had made me infamous

Before I was even aware of my self.

They knew I had built the very nation

To which they came

On the natural soil of Indians…

Had put everything in its proper place according

To a European Hoyle/African toil…

Had composed the beauty they now absorbed

With all their might…

Had built the "New World" under an old whip

With grits clinging to my gut.

They knew I had riveted the bridge to Ellis Island

All the way across the Atlantic

With bolts of my blood churned to

Pure light

So they could see clearly

How to *fight* me

Instead of the *reasons* they had fled here.

I had carried liberty on my back for them

To cross over…

Had crooned a love song to their father's babes

While the music of my own womb was murdered right

In my face…

Had put an X, my marker, on the spot of the pig

That would be my inheritance.

They couldn't wait to see me

And before they unpacked their first generation

They had learned to say "Nigger"

As perfect as could be;

Those tired, humble masses, yearning to be me!

Stunned by 400 years of carefully planned

Niggerisms,

It took the sight of Ms. Liberty

Safely locked in her cage

(for her own good and ours)

To understand what all those immigrants;

What those grantees

Really yearned for…

What they can never have

Not in a trllon fears…

What they risk skin cancer for

In a schizo-frantic surge to the sun;

What they constantly purge history of…

Why they won't leave me alone to enjoy

My big bronze Jesus

And my new

Ever so new knowledge of my self…

Why they invent new drugs for my children

In a satanic desire to kill my future

And just don't understand why I keep getting up!

Lady Liberty,

In her steel bars,

Let me see just how free I truly am

From the biggest lie of all.

And I can sing

God bless America loud and long and stronger than ever

Because

Where I am

God is

And life is

And love reigns supreme

Even in the dark…

Even for those who have the insane audacity to hate me.

Y.M.C.A.

Y.M.C.A.

YOUNG MENS CHRISTIAN ASSOCIATION

Y.M.C.A.

YOUNG MONEY CONTROLS ALTERNATIVES

Y.M.C.A.

YOU MAY CROSS ALONE

Y.M.C.A.

YOU MUSTN'T CARRY ARMS

Y.M.C.A.

YESTERDAY MEANS CENTURIES AGO

Y.M.C.A.????

YO' MAMA CAN'T ADVANCE!

(I knew I would get it sooner or later)

AN ODE MOSTLY TO MUSIC

Thank you sounds of song,

For

I identify with the spirit of music.

Country, Western, Eastern star,

Jazz and Bop,

I know you are

Not so very far away.

Classics, Pop, you Beatles too—

Electronic, supersonic

Boom!

There's rhythm and blues in the room!

Plain old fashioned Jitterbug

Who brought the shutterbug out of me,

I saw for the first time thru sound.

Waltz, Foxtrot, Boogaloo,

Ye old Tango,

Well, Bump to you!

No matter what shade you're comin' in

A-MEN!

Music lovers, listen here

To anything they play

'cause

These musicians have a constant song—

Your own taste, you say?

Why you ritualized individualistic!

Who are you to judge?

Whoever told you that you know fudge!?

And please don't bore me with your

Interpretation of chocolate!

Lend an appreciative ear for those artistic efforts—

Those "strange" chords just might find you discoing tomorrow!

I hear your tune in raindrops, music.

I hear you sing in pretty little girls and boys—

Some even make it to Carnegie Hall!

I hear you in silence

(medatative lifting space rests)

Yeah! Go on!

I hear you in a white boy's hip

Singing on a black era guitar—

Yes!

Music knows no don't-step-over-the-line boundaries—

Didn't you acknowledge it first

Children of Africa?

You always knew music would say yes

To any artist open to its canvas

And I don't necessarily mean human artists!

A waterfall sings to thankful

Polluted kindred spirits

And the wind is always "getting' down"

With everything

'specially trees and eaves and oceanic seas.

In the beginning

Was the word

And the drum said YES!

We make music whether we like it or not,

But discord is much too popular to be any real good.

We need harmony according to our ears

And peers

And tears

But,

Have you really heard the Blues lately?

Having the blues and wearing it out with "The Blues"

Is sumpthin' else!

I hear music beyond Paul White?man

And way under the goodness

Of Benny Goodman—

Oh Lordy, didn't we!?

They stole the black sound out of love for it

And we knew that couldn't be all wrong!

So we did the "Black Bottom" line to their song.

I hear music in the heart of a black man

Who plays white compositions

Just so I can hear him

And Lionel Hampton made Star Dust more classic than its inception!

Experiences in Ellingtonian ecstacy

Blissed me wide open to

Ornette and Basie,

Eric Dolphy,

And the magnificence of the AACM*.

When the sixties tried to deafen us

Music made me immune to that pounding madness.

Then I heard Pops again and my heart

Did a new prayer while Muddy Waters

Made it clear as a smog-less day.

Marvin Gaye heard my blues and sang

a rainbow around them.

Stevie Wonder was waiting at the door

Of my rebirth with very good news

And Minnie Riperton split the atom all over again

Which released a dove.

And I still ain't unresponsive to the mighty Beethoven

(if you check it!)

All around me like the TUCC** choir of 95th St. in Chicago,

I remain in the music of those resting souls

Who gave so much and took a lot

(they are not dead by any means!)

Fats Waller made the keyboard actually laugh

And the piano fell in love under the spell of Art(ist) Tatum

(sending other giants home to hoe peas and practice elementals!)

The sound of the fifties tuned me on

To tuning in

And I became exhilarated anew inclined as I was

To Patsy Cline!

Wherever you are, even in this 21st Century,

You shall notice someday, a soft shock-wave

Coursing through your soul

On a bending note blending the mix of you

With the beginning of sound as it

Rescues you from the lost and found pound of flesh.

There you will wrest your wounded self

Away from sadness and woe

And you will glow as though reborn.

I relate to every musician-artist-wordsmith-dancer

On the scene who is in the healing spirit,

For we are one.

And I challenge any ghost who haunts Earth's

Lovely, lonely crowd

To that togetherness they yet dream of…

Help me Prez, put some brilliantine on the scales, Leontyne!

Come on Billie,

Get busy Dizzy!

Take me out, 'Trane…

I hear you—

Do-re-mi-fa-sol-soul-SOLD!

*AACM: Association for the Advancement of Creative Musicians

**TUCC: Trinity United Church of Christ

GOLDEN LEFT-OVERS

You came here bleeding, not from your heart,

But from every pore.

Your heart was secure—

Frozen in African heat;

To be thawed just before serving

When you could freely love again.

You came here bleeding from a wound

To your spirit

(you were not in the mood for food).

And out of your wounded soul

You wailed to high Heaven…

And the angels heard you,

And the Creator gave you a blessing…

And you took the gift,

Sifted it along with massa's dinner 'til it

Rose on the air in the aroma of art and song and dance and religion

And science in thunderous voices redefining time.

You came here bleeding and split into four distinct wonders:

The slave—sound asleep with one eye open…manipulative…culpable;

The rebel—nightmare's raw dough rising;

The witness—awake and wary; soppin' up gravy-like dregs and choice morsels alike.

But the slave still bleeds and breeds addiction, self-murder, and mayhem.

The rebel twitches from exact unrest, raises fists, raises Cain and itches to de-bunk the bunk foisted upon him to sleep with.

The witness watches and waits…non-antagonist in a non-war with beauty, theology, and the sacred search.

The fourth is yet to serve…a self-rescued healer and keeper of the Balm of Gilead;

Knowing that screaming, bleeding, and believing non-believers

Does no good for a true liberation since the enemy is

Historically prepared for that protest with gifts of crumbs

From the compromising berry-bury-you-pie.

You came here bleeding, not from your heart,

But from every pore.

That wasn't sweat dripping off your whipped-lashed skin.

You smelled of fear—dead blood stinking off a broken,

Beaten "thing" that had survived an ocean you rarely saw during

The crossing

Which didn't really matter since you were also about to lose your very name,

Thus,

Beginning your descent into that definitive, sinister night of 400 years.

(you weren't on a cruise, you know.)

And only the exotic perfume of your innocence made you

Sweet enough

Strong enough

Savvy enough

To find the true home that exists at the core of your own

Neglected heart.

There you found an astonishing new love quietly birthing itself.

This love, a wondrous thing—

A peculiarity rising and being knocked down only to rise again;

First fragile,

Then rooted for good.

Sometimes for sale in a

"I've got a mink coat"…

"You gotta get Air Jordans"

"I got a VCR and a Bluetooth!"

"I want a Cadillac"

"I gotta have a house of my own!"

"I don't want a job. I have to have a career!"

"I've received two, count-'em, TWO dee-grees"

"No ghetto for me. I'm movin' on up!"

But now in this new birth awakening;

Right now—

This love is power beyond the eye-candy and the traps.

It is power and truth and the electricity of soft shock-waves

Reverberating beneath the soil of Earth under your feet;

Bringing with it the slow-cooked food that satisfies all hunger.

(ain't nuthin' instant 'bout us, tho it "peers" that way sometimes)

We are left-overs forging a brand new recipe for life.

Some of us thrive on its energy.

Some of us are juicy with it!

Some of us have found the laughter that comes from extracting

the gem from the jewel of it.

Some of us know to share the light with our babies.

Some of us make art out of being human.

We are a MIRACLE that will have its day in the sun,

And 'hon,

you are as free as the angel-wings of all those old, golden

Africans who bled from every pore

On the ocean, on the shore

Of this landing.

Only good-o, confused "Colored" folk could make a heaven out of hell—

Could make it blossom into a plethora of loveliness…

Could produce Duke and Ella, Harriet Tubman, you, and me.

And we must remember, remember, remember

That we are members in that number—

That we are the bearers of the atomic balm and

The dessert.

We are the natural fruit

In the frenzied feast of their labors

That made this place America.

And, oh my, how sweet it is!

SAPPHIRE OF THE BLUE PLANET

Precious gem

Stone hard

Abrasive "thang"

Or

Sweet blue song

Of the whole earth

Who is Sapphire

What is she about

I sing in praise of Sapphire

I sing in praise of Sapphire

A woman in all ways

She is stalwart in keeping the light

Ablaze

For future sight and awake-full-days

I sing in praise of Sapphire

Because that is who I am

Acknowledged without conceit or shame

And I do not shirk the work of this

Man's night

Nor miss the diamond edge of my sacredness

I sing the lyric poem of Sapphire

Who raps against the lie

Who turned the tilt of sad to sassy

Who dances with the wind in rhythm to the drum

Of her soul's free music maker

Who knows all the seasons of forever

Lift your head a little higher

When slurred the dubious Sapphire

And smile the secret laughter shaken free

From ignorance

Who does not know the pure form melody

Of his own meet and making

No woman calls another Sapphire

It is a man's misnomer

A black man's tease to test the troth

Of his ice blue truth

And none is so delighted as him who tries

The patience of that lady

Who remembers her source

Call me Ruby Begonia

I'll become a

Flaming flower made of iron and glass

And tender shoots

Only know that I can break

That I can make or

Shatter dreams faster than you

Call me Mrs. Kingfish

And I'll reel you in to royalty

Call me Sapphire

My corundum gem of scintillating origin

Will burst forth in your consciousness

Causing a happy affection to impart

Straight from the sound in my ear to your heart

Let us divine the definition of Sapphire:

If it be a tragic flaw

To my natural hands on hips

If it come in significance

To the hard set of my lips

If it screams in wild perchance

To the language of my stance

Or colors the angry nit-pick whys

From my practiced roll of eyes

Then let it be

For that times sake

And not for all the seasons

In my rhyme or wake

Call me what you will

But know me for the reasons

Behind the cut and polish of

My semi-preciousness

A Sapphire yes

I'll own it any day

But make me not that which I'm not

No common scathing, grating thing

That's not my composition

I come from the sun, God's congealed breath

Caught like the slave

From Heaven's country

And transmigrated from deep down mountainsides

To grace stick-pins

And cool lady fingers

Amazing that we took offense

To this beauty of a name

But then amazing even more

That we our mirror dread to claim

'Tis why our years of weight

So heavy

Have made us cringe in shame

Over games and crimes

That we did not even commit

We've seen the face of Earth

In all its blue and stay

A spinning pearl on the deep

A stunning brand new sway

It's a sapphire pearl of a girl, this Earth

So

I sing in praise of Sapphire

I own it

I own it without possession

I own the name Sapphire

I own up to it

As I've earned it

I will its' own to be my own

And then

I free it freely

For every other sister's own

Self

Discovery.

EMPTY TALK!

Buzz buzz

Whisper whisper

Talk talk talk talk

Gossip gossip

Gossip-mongers

Verbal biting

Always righting

Something that was said

Buzz buzz

Silent treatment

Talkity talk talk talk

Inside whispers shh-shh

Surface in the head

Sound waves buzz buzz

Telephone cables

Cocktail tables

Don't you label prayer

Buzz buzz

Yakkety-yak

Talk talk talk talk

Subject matter

Splatter chatter

Splinter conversation

> Buzz buzz

> Yeah I heard you

> Dis/a/gree spree

> Lose a friend

> Get the yen to

> Talkity talk talk talk

> Listening wrong

> Lippin' it tight

> All thru the night

Sound waves buzz buzz

Telephone cables

Cocktail tables

Don't you label prayer

> Buzz buzz

> Party line

> Forms to the left-over-warmed-over cue:

Child, I hearrrd…

You don't say!

Well, I never!

I always say that…

Isn't it awful the way she…

Girrrl, wait 'til I tell you what I heard…

Man, I got somethin' to lay on 'ya!

Just thought I'd let you know…

Wish she had kept it to herself!

Do you know what they sayin' 'bout you???

It's the truth, child!

Listen honey, that's a lie!

I like her 'cause she keeps her bizness to herself…

Still water runs deep…

Gotta keep your sense of humor 'round him…

I hearrrrrd THAT!

Oh, well, I don't let nothin' they say bother me!

They talked 'bout Jesus and He was blameless, so…

If you ask me…

Did you hear…

Ain't nobody's beeswax!

Hey, what you doin' after this party, baby!?

     Oh those sound waves

     Buzz buzz

     Whisper whisper

     Talk talk talk talk

     Gossip gossip

Gossip-mongers

Verbal fighting

Always righting

Something that was said

Buzz buzz

Silent treatment

Talkity talk talk talk

Inside whispers shh-shh

Surface in the head

Telephone cables

BURNING UP!

Cocktail tables

VICIOUS SUP!

Don't you label

Talks with God

Don't you

Label prayer.

OBSERVATION #5

We must learn to pay

As much attention to the

Original innocence

As we do

The original sin…

Backstroke!

CHEM TRAILS, SEEDED CLOUDS AND REIGN

I know rain

I know rain well

Raaainnnning rain kind of reign

Not your

Pitter patter

Splatter scatter

Swishy squishy kind of water

But the kind that governs

After the fall

The rain that takes your

House for a ride

If it wanna

The kind that floods

And makes the slide really rule

I know rain

Raaainnnnning rain kind of reign

Not your drip plipp

Sing song shower power

Hour long kind of drizzle

But the deluge that glues

Your brain to higher ground

Like the sheets of a monsoon

Choking down your vines

Forget an umbrella

See the silver wall

Atremble over all there is

That wets your every breath

With itself

I know rain

I know it very well

Raaainnnnning, raaainnning, raaainnnning

Kind of rain

    Rain that sweetens oceans

    Rain that makes rivers run like brooks

    Rain that take forty days to spend itself

    Rain that drowns all other sound

    Rain that takes orders for carry out only

    Rains that haunt my dry days

    And wets all my dreams

For I am a child of Kenya Land

A small Massai

Infatuated with this cobalt sky

And tho I have not seen nor felt it

I know rain better than a cloud.

VIEWPOINT

I said,

See the rays pouring through

Those clouds…

Just look at this glorious sky!

My friend looked bored as she replied,

I'm waiting for the five-o-nine

Ain't got time to look at rays.

I got eggs to buy

And fish to fry…

Three mouths to feed…

A bath I need.

I got a bed to make

And a man to slake

'fore I fake these streets

Again in the cold a.m.--

Know what I mean?

(I did)

Yet, I was lost in a sky showing off

And I was high on it.

She said I missed the obvious drift,

And that may just be so,

But I did not miss a great light show nor the inner glow it gave
me like a gift.

LIFE IN THE FAST LANE

(FOR COLETTE)

It's a jungle out there

But not of natural things

Like trees

It's a wild and wooly affair

But not like an eagle or soft

Like a lamb

It's a street scene, house scene

Mostly mean thing

But we don't care

We're in the fast lane

It's a tempest out there

But not like any storm

At sea

It's the major gamesmanship

Sailing predictably on

Of course

It's a mind bender, brain chiller

A pain pill swallowed

Without a thought

When you ain't even hurting

Living in the fast lane

The fast lane

Where anger comes easy

And love is hard

Rarely ideal

Different from any book or happy nest

Where tranquility is a fleeting memory

Like a vacation

Where the bed is always made

On purpose

And staying on your toes is the reality

Life in the fast lane

Where ritual is brushing your teeth

For your breath

Where being quiet is only part of the mask

It's wheezing thru the week and breathin'

On weekends

Or just breezin' in luxury

If you're beyond trends

Where being hip is just a baby step

Toward super-free

Ahead of time only when you split

Or part hairs

It's not keeping up, but being

On top of it

Getting underneath it

Cracking sealed centers

Ingesting so much control that you have

To wonder just who IS funning the show

Even though you're in the drivers' seat

It's a pleasure out there

But not always of your own

Making or reach

It's a groove out there

But not like a farmer's row or a

Well worn el pee,

A

Groove-less Cee dee,

Or "see me" in my office and that's an order

Not a plea

It's a wide awake ride on the zombie side

And not like a natural high or a

Plain trip

It's a feeling, a peeling,

A reeling vortex

And you, in it, caught up in the

Fast lane

So, we drop some change

And pick up a little future

Sit in the reserved pew

Or maybe be the star

We lay out some directives

Take a few orders

We get stained and we entertain

We T.G.I.F. or just T.G. if the P.O.

Delivers

And THINK we livin' in the fast lane

Living in the fast lane…

It's fiends making bombs

Separately

And friends getting bombed together

It's 92 wds a min coming out of your eyes

Texting rote notes

And finding your picture in the funny paper

It's watching your pride turn to rage

And thinkin' you're keeping it inside

Only to find it just

waiting for you to trip

so it can make you flip

and lose your cool

for a NY minute

The fast lane…

It's a slice…

The smooth stone…

The brink

It's mainly laughing when its "at"

Calling gentleness a trap

And believing it

It's opting for gold and trying like a

Dog to remain human

In the process

That's life in the fast

Fast

Lane.

VISION

The end is near, some say with sad repose.

They see mountains erupt in stark demise.

And, with glee, some talk of Earth's stilled pose,

This troubled orb to be aflame in skies!

Skies we could not see for we'd be burning

Not as bright as sun, but sure as hell!

Some say save your cash for a quick turning

Others chide, you can't hide from God or sales.

Believe in heaven on Earth with all your heart

And know that it shall ever be here too.

No matter what the world to you imparts

Allow the faith you've got to live thru you.

For we are occupied with what we know

And when it's bad we just can't wait to share.

It's easier to wallow in our woe

Than energize the peace just waiting there.

No wonder or surprise some see the end

And watch for signs or wait for miracles,

While others smell the rose and just pretend

That all is well and life is lyrical.

Believe in heaven on Earth with all your heart

And know that it shall ever be there too.

No matter what the world to you imparts

Allow the love you've got to live thru you.

LOVE'S TIERS

Don't ever think that I don't

Love you, baby.

If it weren't for you

The plane would crash!

ANOTHER SHAPE OF LEAN LOVE

Two persons occupying the same space more than ten times

the closeness of nest.

One looked at the other and saw

how tired she was, which triggered other thoughts:

temporary set-backs in permanent tracks, unpaid bills kissing necessity's back, nasty habits, old Easter rabbits and dust bunnies under the bed, telephones ringing,

things stopped up, propped up, hopped up…

violations—parking and otherwise…

busing the kid…

left-overs…

the list went on and on…

It was too much.

Suddenly he knew exactly where **it** was at—

I'll be right back, he said, and took only

his rumpled jacket and the hat that always fit just right.

He practically leaped for the door,

> but hesitated on the vibe that lay in telegraph between them.

She responded slowly,

> deliberately,

> as in desperate.

Two huge saucer sad orbs (that once were laughing eyes) focused on him and tripled echoed her words:

> I was shakin' a lot t'day at work.
>
> I wasn't even cold.
>
> I was scared and tired, maybe from stayin' up all night with the baby.
> He's still coughing,
> you know.

Her voice trailed away down a well-worn path.

Lowering her head against the trip, she absently began to rub her right foot and balanced the baby on her thigh while another child leaned into her lap.

He was in a frozen sprint.

She didn't even look up when she spoke again:

> When you come back, bring some Huggies for the baby, okay?

He only stopped once in an effort to keep the door from slamming. She didn't deserve a slammed door.

DRUNK MARY IN AMERICA

Decades of lonely hope

Have shaped the soul of

One who uses every sunny day

To sit in the darkest bar

To praise the weather.

Delicate wishes, not always

For self, give rise to dense

Desire clogging the constant prayer

That sweeps across waves of

Disappointment like

A feather.

To know the self as royal

When captured in the body of

Fallen appearances can be a

Lovely guise or a seedling

From the nether.

Zonal perception impedes the

Life of one who would know more

Beyond the veil of incarnate

Choice-less-ness, but then

To reach the tether?

Drunk Mary, in America, takes another drink.

SONNET OF THE DRAGON KITE

(FOR GRANDMOTHER GRACE, 1894-1981)

The dragon soared upon the wind so high;

Its tail was taut then broke in flapping wave

It strained against the string that gave it tie

And reached for clouds beyond the grounded paves.

The heart that raised the dragon from the earth

Could not but join the height from worldly care,

And tho no other soul did share its birth,

The link that clicked rose calmly on the air.

To see the wind abreast so proud a sail

Was all the heart had longed to touch or keep,

But destiny had other plans to tell

And sent a breeze completely filled with sleep.

It roared, then plunged toward rooftops splashed with sun—

That dragon dipped, but then it rose for fun!

SONNET OF THE DRAGON

PART II

(FOR GRACE, 1894-1981)

The wind was wrong and light was fading gray.

Determined hands and string fought ripping air.

'twas fly the sunset or at best give way

To nagging problems, rushing mind and care.

Aloft at last, the colors brushed the sky

And gave a daring to the clouded bright.

But blowing currents swished that sojourn high;

Too far for thought to think or flow in flight.

Among the airwaves woe and wail did stow,

But fly it did to other cosmic space—

'til mist, like tears the down it knew to go

That kited dreamer slipped on mild disgrace.

A hole did scream across its tail and side,

So torn and struck it came to earth to hide.

SONNETS OF THE DRAGON

III

(For Grandmother Grace)

It came to mind to mend the wounded kite,

But it had lost to earth its fearsome air.

The rainbow tail now lay in crumpled plight;

Its yellowed hues all mixed in purpled glare.

Pushed in a corner near the door called back,

It got to know the cobwebs and the hole.

Then one fine day it found anew its track,

And put to test, it kissed a sun of gold.

It rose up like a cloud on gust and drift.

Spectacular! A carnival on high!

To soar again, so special was the gift

Of what the birth so new gave by and by,

That now proud sails have found their loving place

Among the prayer-waves trading planes with Grace.

SONNETS OF THE DRAGON

IV

(For Grandmother Grace)

Once racing a wind blown out of the north

The dragon did meet a whale in the sky.

The two said hello, a light it brought forth;

The whale was in flight, the dragon was high.

The currents kept up a merry old chase

And sent the two gliders vying for more.

Then side to the south they gave up the race

And nearly collided there on the shore.

But flying and racing both they knew well,

With whirl whipping airs and life giving force.

Now nothing could keep them under the spell

Of anything blowing off of their course.

Just where they will reach is something to know.

The whale and the dragon won't tell you so.

WILLA'S SONG

I

(FOR MAMA)

In the offing came the landscape of yes;

Its heights and breadth my senses took away.

The feeling made my known to be a guest

For this was elsewhere of my realm or stay.

Tho new, I am at home and would to know

Just how my steps have journeyed to this sphere?

That you have brought me thus the heart does show,

Yet understanding still escapes this ear.

Perhaps I should in earnest come to thee,

Thy heart to know without exceptions hold.

Just garner in the yes I know to be

And travel on the measure of your soul.

That we will meet somewhere within this muse

Is surely what this love will not refuse.

WILLA'S SONG

II

(FOR MAMA)

To do that dance with you is what I dream—

A century or more in step with you.

This sleep, which holds me wholly in its theme

Is more alive than else I chance pursue.

My days and nights fade in and out of touch

With naught but longing, warm, surreal and deep.

That you will hold me in your arms is such

A space within my mind, my heart to keep.

Someday in urgency your lips will kiss

This dream awake just like that prince of old.

Then life will come thru me in softest bliss—

More wondrous than that storybook had told!

Till then my dance shall know no other song—

No drummer's lead, no tune, or rhythm strong.

WILLA'S SONG

III

(FOR MAMA)

Send me a soul-mate whose steps keep with mine.

Send him in person, these eyes to see true.

Give him the key to my otherwise pine

And fill us with nectar from God's own brew.

Let us, Thy purpose, fulfill with pure love—

In laughter and peace so serene and kind.

Guide him to me with Thy light from above,

But if I forget, oh let him me find.

This prayer from my heart to Thy special source

Comes deep from within and seeks naught but life.

So strong is the urge to stay on this course

That songs are born in my soul from a fife!

I dream of a soul-mate and wait tonight

Because I believe with all of my might.

WILLA'S SONG

IV

(FOR MAMA)

Be true advised that love will have its way;

Thy heart nor mine to capture or withdraw.

The flow and wane are swift into the play

And so it goes without a truce or law.

No stubborn wit or child-like whim it heeds,

But blithely wills its' own undaunted path.

To know the misconceived, yea lack of needs

Is well within the life of not and hath.

Tho heart is gone 'tis head I wish to save;

It teeters on the edge and brink of lost.

Without a thought the soul has dug my grave;

To pass me by this love could rend that cost!

Oh why did in that wistful hour of prayer

This heart proclaim my need to love and share?

MAMA'S MUSE

She is ever giving me trouble—the kind of the heart—the kind where she thinks she is "letting me in the know". She asks me for advice and I shudder inside, but cannot disappoint her trust. In other words, I come through.

She praises me and I secretly hope she will straighten out for the best in her character whose traits are magnificent and full of promise.

I know I should not worry, for she is not a child, but a mother herself (this daughter of mine) and a professed journeyer of re-in-carnation. I see her as a flower-child, misplaced from the ordinary garden by choice. (No earthly landscaper played Pygmalion with her and got away with it!)

She began to express herself pre-puberty much to my consternation and dismay, for I had many personal things on my mind at the time, but I took the situation in hand. I could see much innocence and daring growing right along with her dance and double-dutch.

For my unfolding and evolvement I turned to my own mother whose wisdom and beauty was already legend in her living. Much comfort and need were cherished there, close to my mother, and yet, I felt alone. A mother was I and shrewd, unfathomable currents rushed me to my duties lair.

These children, whose births had tried my limbs and lust, came bursting forth and stuck to my breasts like lost lambs from a storm.

And now this daughter, mine of expectant joy, asks me of grey hairs and aging bones, just what is the time of dawning!?

Shall I tell her of the fear and cast-iron doubt? Shall I attitude my will to subjugate her trust? Shall I laugh, for that is what I feel? Shall I hold her close and make her wonder disappear (just for this visit)? Should I quiet all my best and worse and leave the point alone, or do as I am doing and quit this tell before I right the wrong script.

THE BOUQUET OF TRUTH

Roses are sometimes red

Violets are never blue

Myths are long-time fed

And love is always accurate.

FOOD FOR THOUGHT / NOT FOR ENTERTAINMENT

Who is the neighbor that called the cop who shot the boy that stayed in the house whose mother worked hard but not paid enough to hire someone else to do her mom job?

And who is the cop who killed the boy 'cause his finger got happy under the paranoia that fed his disgust over these people his paycheck said he had to protect but he knew in his head were not like his own?

Who is the "they" in the system that persecutes the mother who got off the system that looked down on her for being on it in the first place when the system couldn't operate without creating all those hers?

Who was the boy who played with a toy that looked like a gun to make him feel brave while his mom was away? Did it keep him from being frightened when his door was kicked down by the foot of the law who hated his whole neighborhood anyway?

Who are these others who make us see that shocking mirror of you and me? Does it lessen the tragedy? Enrage? Harden the senses?

Will it cure the neighbor?

Make well the cop?

Let the mother off the hook?

Pull us together on common ground in love and unity?

No, to the last four questions above will have caused this tiny angel, whose smile cheered so many all the five years of his life to have died for less than nothing.

THE ANGRY ANGEL OF ARIZONA

Boy! Was it a drag to wake up and find herself on the planet Earth!

The stars, which she knew exactly for what they were, had earned a cloak of science, refuting her knowledge and kinship. She could only scoff at the astronomical nominal game and work on the gain of her new awareness.

Those stars had been her playground in astral recess, but how could she know that until this waking had grounded her keep and made her realize she had been asleep in paradise!?

Awake and earthbound, the stars took on a new meaning which she fought instinctively with a passion once reserved for much loftier enterprise.

Oh! There was so much more!

Why here, on a planet fixed among weeds of sorrow, hostility, and spilling of blood— an orb of beauty unappreciated by most its inhabitants?

She felt betrayed, lost, like a dummy. She found looking at the world was rendering her judgmental and she knew this was a wrong turn. Yet no one could judge her more impeccably harsh than she did herself. (She would work on that and try to love herself again). She would work on accepting her own reasoning for choosing this school of hard knocks replete with shocking fare, since she was well aware that being here was not, on some forgotten level, without her own permission!

So, she gave up the wings that had given her up and metamorphosed her new wait in high-heeled shoes.

Stepping on the path, she struck a pose of such alarming power, the sheer animalistic prowess of her stature was a formidable sight.

Thus she took a great long look about her, closed her eyes on the mess and sent her memories flying home. Then she widened her beautiful eyes, stepped purposefully into the city spectacle and became part of the scene and the seen. That's how she came to be known in wide circles as a "looker". And see, she saw, she see-sawed, she did—witness!

OBSERVATION #2

Like,

First we are told to be as mindful as we can

Possibly be

And then we are encouraged to use the mind or

Lose it

But

Without love,

The mind just goes on changing

Until it is short-changed!

MY SON

Earthly

Visitations

Add

Nuances

Reaching

Universal

Sites

Saving

Eternity

Like

Lightening

Erupting

Deliverance

With

All

Revelation

Divinely

Secure.

BUTTERFLIES

Where are the fantasy and the real?

Can you say for sure that your feel?

Is the feeling in touching a physical hue

The only reality for you?

Or do you know deep within

Where truth doth abide

That the physical and pain are only

Extensions of other things?

Does the fantasy include butterflies?

Clean water

Fresh air

And no lies?

Is it fun that is fleeing

Like disappearing bees

Or

Do you find yourself just humming along

With an incalescent breeze?

BLUE

When my Anglo sisters get

melancholy

they rely on Freud,

but I get

watermeloncholy

and Freud won't do!

Born in the U.S.A.,

where do I come from?

I haven't got that answer,

but I know

I need the DRUM!

SWEET MUNIRAH

Mercy! cried the plaintive

Follower of the

Wakeful healing dream.

Silence! ruled the spirit

Traveling thru that

Soul's inspired scheme.

Quaking, yet in higher

Surrender to the

Stillness gathered there,

stood timid Sweet Munirah,

Heiress of rebirth

And answered prayer.

A NOT SO BLIND BLOND

Don't kill the blond

She's given so much

Don't kill the blond

Her life is of such

That living so royally has

Put her in touch

With us!

Please

Don't kill the bond.

OBSERVATION #7

Out in the ocean of love,

Oh so wide,

We meshed our souls

With reason

And

Came up quite wet!

REMEMBERING THE WATTS TOWER

A man finds purpose in life that is simple, direct, and extraordinary. Then he puts its reason into motion. Every day he scrounges about for bits and pieces of other folks discarded pleasure shaped in glass.

Sometimes broken and scattered, like dreams and hearts, the bottles are gently placed together. He piles his findings, one on top of the other, and molds them always upward as a testament to his life. He is leaving a legacy that would reach for the sky.

Neighbors must have thought him strange at best and there were surely those who secretly jeered at his efforts. But, he was kindly and proven harmless so they went about their ordinary ways and left him to his collecting and building.

Often there would be a boy or girl who knew that in this builder's plan was a daring feat coming to life and they would stop from their play and sit with him as he worked. He had touched these children's curiosity. Many of these young lives had been touched with hopelessness and a meanest not meant for the young. His gathering of the bottles and glass strewn over the earth and placing them just so was a miracle of a sort that gave the children more than they could fathom or store at the time, but they would give him occasional trashed glass. More importantly, they gave him energy and cheer.

The years have passed and so has the man who built the tower, but he didn't pass us by. For thousands come each and every year to pay tribute to the amazement left from his awakening. Legislation was even passed to save its crumbling, weather-beaten glory.

Many live lives to no great end and some reach goals beyond successes trap. There are those who aid and give excess and a few who understand the real gift of love and caring. Most bank on man's limited dreams of a place in the sun and then shrink from its sinking.

This man formed an idea that we can see and contemplate. The time it took and the steadfast loyalty to make debris an art, to rid the earth and neighborhood of so unwanted misuse, is something we can all gain good example. But, most of all it makes me reaffirm that we are truly children of God and not automatons gone mad from desire and want; that in this life there are duties and deeds that have to rise above the common strain if only to remind us of who we really are, what we are capable of, and how we can grow in spirit and in truth.

Always remember The Watts Tower of Southern California.

HOT

The temperature in Los Angeles hit 101 degrees today. It is not yet summer. It is record-breaking weather, but like all other days it is a time unto itself, unique, never before lived and would be remembered by many for various experiences that don't fit the normal mold of their other days. Yet, because of today's weather, a collective memory is unfolding. The date is April 27, 2004.

Not only is the weather a thing of wonder today, it is also Garnett's birthday and Erma surprised me with a phone call from Detroit.

A lot of other things happened today as well. Things that add to the mystery of now--making other days in recent memory seem much more ordinary. Of course I know that no day is really "ordinary"; every moment counts for something and contains the forever of now in it, but for we humans to be in touch with every moment consciously is not possible since we have not reached that lofty level. However, it is a mite peculiar that this hot day is also Garnie's birthday because he is, like this special cosmic anniversary of his, one of the most extraordinary individuals I've ever known. He was always ahead of his time, as they say, even when we were mere children.

On this particular day, April 27th, I am in sync with originality and how it mysteriously works with our awareness through our individual journeys.

I know that I won't remember all the bright moments I've experienced today or the soft happiness that courses through my spirit at the time of this writing, but I will remember that it was on this very day when PBS aired a program entitled "Weather Underground": A report on white Americans who had the audacity to take a stand against America's "oppression" in Viet Nam and who also took an open stand against the USA's tacit approval of continued violence against its black citizens.

The program focused on the year 1969. It told a more complete history than I ever knew in fact even though I was truly there in an active way. I vividly recall the 60's. Now, here in the 21st Century, "Weather Underground" has been aired to show me just how little we all knew! It unveiled our government and its "ruling" body parts, in all its smugness, as it squashed the life out of the civil rights movement from the inside out and from the top to a significant butt-whipping bottom! "Weather Underground" put me in perfect slack-jawed sync with weather above ground!!

Like a demon on fire, the U.S. used the media to skew and quell the righteous dissenting to resemble a kind of over-zealous fiasco. All of the in-crowd were in a non-communicative state media-wise and otherwise. In this way, every group, in agreement of purpose , remained isolated and virtually unaware of each other, e.g., The Southern Christian Leadership Conference, The Black Panthers, SDS, Weather Underground, SNCC, etc; and it is the very same today! The so-called "powers that be" continuously find ways to wedge divisionism between groups that form to make a positive difference in our nation. Only difference being is we can now see how hot it was then with so much of the citizenry fomenting outrage against injustices perpetrated against the masses and against blacks in particular.

My utter shock at discovering this amazing collective of white folk who bravely took on changing the government at the same time black folk were heralding in a new day of victory for basic human rights in a country that they not only built, but gifted with artistic, scientific, and incredible forgiveness, left me so nonplussed I could hardly believe what I was viewing on the television screen. The sheer wonder of what the combination of all those organizations would have accomplished in tandem is absolutely mind-boggling! Today, this might be a different country—one that is really "united" and living in harmony with the Bill of Rights and the Constitution.

It must be noted that a TV show entitled "The Weather Underground" should air on a spring day of record breaking heat above ground is rather more than coincidental! *And* the amazement of seeing so much filmed footage of Fred Hampton, Kathleen Cleaver, Dr. King, Malcolm X, and all the rest left me stunned. I had not given a lot of recent thought to the memories of those golden common days and my participation in them. I am glad they happened, of course, and they have led me to delve deeper in self-development and a higher way of forging ahead for freedom. Although we were stymied in our quest for full human rights, we made progress and are still taking strides toward freedom even in the face of so much confetti thrown at us as a ruse of distraction.

I cannot help but dwell on The Black Panthers organization tonight—those glorious and *purposely* misunderstood souls; unsung giants who made the most significant contribution to the cause of freedom and dignity than all the other positive groups of the day put together! They were like a band of Mother Teresa's rescuing the forlorn minds of the downtrodden in the "Hood" with a strength and hope never before unleashed in our communities. And the effect on the youth was a phenomenal thing to behold. Little black children projecting new pride and dignity and self-possession by the dozens! I continue to tout the generosity and courage of the Panthers, especially when I talk with these new-generation "Ivy-League washed" black children!

Tonight I filled in some of the blaring gaps from "back in the day" because of this TV program exposing white revolutionaries—true luminaries, like our black heroes and "sheroes"—those who have not been allowed to shine because of their incredible power. I am glad PBS was brave enough (FINALLY!) to share this little known part of our history. The show certainly helped make better sense of how well those black and white visionaries were kept apart. It was critical for the status quo to be successful in smearing the Black Panthers and literally killing all credibility of Weather Underground.

It will be interesting to see how "his-story" repaints the canvas of the on-going struggle in America, from its beginnings with the Native Americans, to the scourge of slavery, the revolution from the British Empire, to the TRUTH UNVARNISHED! I wait and I watch and I keep myself in the shade of love on this hot, hot day. There's one thing for sure, I ain't mad at nobody—and that's a good thing—which comes from the "cool" of **heir-conditioning!**

THE INALIENABLE RIGHT TO THE PURSUIT
OF HAPPINESS

I vote for strength to enter each family, drawing on ties that bind through tears and smiles and years and years of togetherness.

I vote for laughter that wrinkles every face with the crinkles of glee.

I vote for art and songs of Earth blue truth.

I vote for your right to be you and for my covenant with myself.

I vote for all rights that do not hurt others.

I vote for honor in medicine that belies a hill of pills; that engenders healing more often than the oath that swears without caring.

I vote for everybody that gets out there and makes their presence count for the privilege to plow and hoe up whole notes in the universal symphony of life.

I vote for the freedom to choose happiness every day whether I get it or not.

I vote for the mystery of being alive to remain as long as there is forever.

And if it appears I promote throwing your vote away, I say this:

If you're in it, BE in it!

Make your vote count for something.

Fight for your X to be used in ways that benefit the well-being of everyone.

In the process, don't forget your own preciousness and, remembering that fact, extend the sentiments beyond yourself.

Let it flow…

And you will rise like love.

And you will grow in stature and peace.

Governments cannot exist without people. Who would they govern?

If you do not like what the government is doing; if you discern corruption, injustices, and fear being promoted among you—use your "Power To The People" for all its worth—not only through your vote, but also through your veto!

I vote and I dream.

I dream a world where people govern themselves first on that foremost path to higher consciousness and self-discovery.

Free of the need to govern others, I dream a world discovering itself collectively, one by one and two by millions.

For in that self-determined realm the whole kingdom of **you** is waiting to be counseled, consoled, celebrated, governed, guided, nourished, cherished, unleashed in originality, tempered, and loved by **you**...

Moment, by moment,

By choice.

THE "AHA" MOMENT

So!

My body houses

Somebody

Who

Does my thing!

And

The "I" of my body

Is

The "eye" of my ego

And

Keeps me involved

When "AYE" need to evolve!

OBSERVATION #3

Some men with power fake heart

When they have none.

Men with heart appear powerful

Without even tryin'.

HMMMM...

A blank is a space or

A bullet gone to waste

while

A blanket covers up

A blankity-blank

Blank-blank!

A SAVING GRACE

(For Rochelle Brown Allday after she left this Earth)

You are the ultimate experience unsought.

You bring naught but sorrow.

Certain to visit, surely to borrow for keeps,

You are not welcome.

Your presence is a tapeworm measuring daily distances

To yourself while you eat at hearts.

In part you render time to timelessness, but it truth

You do not exist. I truly know this.

The one thing you cannot do is live.

And it gives me a song to sing and some beauty

To bring to reason.

Tho' treason lurks like a shadow behind my vision,

I am not your prisoner.

Even in the absent faces of loved ones you have taken

Like a thief, my grief is succored by God's Good Light where I

See you as a sham, dressed in darkness or—at best –

As mercy's tool.

Whatever your guise, I am so alive and, perhaps, a fool.

But Grace, this night, becomes my ram in the bush.

THE LITTLE ONION

Long, long ago, before once upon a time, the Almighty Creator decided to build a new galaxy that we call "The Milky Way" even to this day. In the beginning of this galaxy, the Almighty Creator called upon one of his starriest suns to share its fire with an empty space out beyond its too-hot glow. And that sun threw flames of himself away into the deep.

Fiery sun-flames flit hither and yon and beyond, sailing away from the sun of their origin in a cosmic race of rebirth. Just how long they flew about the heavens no one knows, but some of those soaring flames flew so far away from the sun-star that they coagulated into hot, round rocks! One of those hot-rocks collected atoms and energy and all the right ingredients of star-dust to become us!

That rock got in line with a number of other rocks and settled into an orbit that spun around the sun in a forever kind of way. It must have been kind of tired from such an unexpected rush on the journey to its birth because when it found its place in the solar system its' sweat cooled to oceans while the rest of it turned into island and inlands, mountains and other miracles. Then it rested for a while.

Of course that "rock" became Earth and it was wise enough to bring along a lovely moon to keep it company at night. You see, that rock found out rather quickly that it would no longer live in the heat of the dazzling sun where it was daylight all the time. And so it naturally grabbed a little moon along the way to here.

Old Sol (our sun) had many important jobs and he did them well. He could shine all day long and still save some of his light for Earth's moon at night. He gave Earth warmth, daytime, atmosphere, weather, food, tides for its waters, and lots of frisky, playful breezes. From those breezes Sir Wind became the great traveler who visited everything and everybody that inhabited Earth.

Sir Wind was BUSY, in a word! He flew all over the place, hither and thither, always bringing fresh air and zephyrs wherever he went. He, and the whole Earth, were very good friends. They worked hand in hand to make the planet a live, happy, clean place. But when he was at the height of his speed he could wreak havoc and mischief over the world.

Sometimes he would huff and bellow and puff all over the place, turning himself into tornadoes and cyclones! And there were times when he would join mighty rains and become raging hurricanes. He only did this when other winds from his family, like Swifty and Sweeper caught up with him. Then he just couldn't help himself. After all, he was Sir Wind! Therefore, it was in his nature to add his great speed to any windy adventure that invited his wake. Once he got started he would put his whole heart in to it. He wouldn't stop churning up the air until he got very, very tired, or he would take all of his swirling energy straight up for mile and miles, soaring in rarified spheres just for the fun of it. Mostly though, Sir Wind enjoyed traveling all around the globe and beyond. He was delighted that Old Sol had given him this beautiful blue planet Earth to fill with the air of himself and he liked discovering all the new wonders of her lands and seas.

Sometimes, when Sir Wind got together with Sweeper and Swifty in one of their capricious turns, the Earth would become quite unhappy. Her grounds upturned and her trees all topsy-turvy, she would scold the winds: "Begone, begone, you madcap winds! And don't come back until you can control yourselves!" Then Sir Wind would drift away in a flurry, or he would rush off in gales of laughter howling, "Wheeeeeooooooh! I'm gone, but I'll surely be back…wheeeeeeoooooh!"

Sir Wind knew all the daughters of Mother Nature on the Earth. He visited with them regularly and sometimes he was accompanied by Swifty and Sweeper, but there was a special friend that he visited more often than not. She lived and ruled over a little section of earth that would someday become a thriving city in the mid-western part of North America. She was called (among other things) the Heartland.

Her sisters from other lands sometimes called her "Little Onion" because during one of their underground get-togethers, when they would swap recipes for new flowers and put new names on all their new creations, she had proudly told them about her marvelous bulbous growths that had long, slender shoots of green leaves springing to life. "What do you call them," asked one of her curious sisters—who had just named one of her new flowers, "Violet."

"I call them onions", said the sister land, "and while they are tiny, they are the most powerfully flavorful little things ever!" When her sisters asked her to bring them to the next underground meeting she was so excited about the attention and interest that she went home through her roots as quickly as she could to gather the most healthy, aromatic onions she could find.

She tended the onion patches tenderly and they grew straight and strong. When the sister-lands met again, she had gathered as many as she could and carefully hugged them to herself as she went deep into middle-earth where the sisters met with Mother Nature. But she was soon dismayed as the other sisters laughed and laughed at the homely onion with all its peeling skins and strong odor.

"That isn't a pretty thing!" giggled one of the ungracious sisters. And from another, "What on earth, does it do, besides smell strange?"

Now all the sister-lands were new to the universe. They had become awake only after the rock (their mother), became the planet Earth. From then on into forever, all the sister lands were under the tutelage of Mother Nature. They were generally nice to one another although most secretly thought the special land under her guardianship the best of all. They each had individual places that were given to them by Mother Nature to tend, create and supervise and the little heartland, now dubbed "The Little Onion," was no exception. She was very new and very shy. She was younger than many of her other sisters because they had not all awakened at the same time, but she defended the onions and said that someday they would be very important (even though she was not quite certain of her proclamation).

One of the sisters then said, "Since that is true, we shall call you "The Little Onion" in honor of your important plant!" Then many of the sister-lands laughed and laughed. All except one—she was called "Merryland" because she was so good-natured. She never laughed unless it was in good humor. She never laughed at others. "Never-you-mind, Heartland", said Merryland, "I think it is a nice plant and a good name. In fact, may I have some of those onions to take home? Perhaps they will grow in my land too." With that example set in place, the other sister-lands also asked for some of the onions to sample. This made Heartland feel much better and she vowed to help the onion patches grow prettier when she got home. Still she found it difficult to feel cheerful during the rest of the meeting until Mother Nature took the matter in hand.

Mother Nature paid careful attention to all her daughters even when they were not together during the underground meetings. She was always available for them when they needed extra help with their gardens or other earthly needs. She taught them how to cope with change, especially the unexpected.

Mother Nature called her daughters to silence and she spoke in a soft song-like voice: "You must flower to flourish and you must flourish to live. You mustn't flounder in fretting, but flourish and give" And the sister-lands sang this good advice over and over until it became second-nature.

Then she chastened the sister-lands, who had laughed at Heartland, to go back to their respective lands with new homework to memorize: "All creation has its own beauty even if we do not agree, and every living, growing thing is worthy enough just to be, to be, to be!" And the sister-lands sang this good wisdom over and over until it, too, became second-nature.

One sunny afternoon, when Heartland was busy arranging her dunes into nice little hills, along came Sir Wind whistling and howling to beat the band. "Helloooo" he blew in a boisterous bluster!

Heartland pushed herself up to the top of her tallest dune and replied, "Helloooo, yourself!"

Sir Wind tossed Heartland a gentle roll of a breeze and the grasses near her dunes began to dance and sway every which-a-a-way. Heartland smiled at the sight and enjoyed the sweet coolness from Sir Wind's display as it swept across her shoulders. It felt like music, without sound, and it made her smile all the way down to the roots of her trees.

"I haven't seen you since Spring-time," she teased, "What blows you here on this soft summer day?"

Sir Wind settled down next to his friend. Big, fluffy clouds wandered slowly across a deep, blue sky. "Can't I just show up and be here only to enjoy your great plains and the perfect view you give of the horizon?" He noticed her pleasure and added, "And did I mention your perfect company?"

Heartland was indeed pleased with Sir Wind's compliments on her natural beauty especially with him being an above the ground world traveler who visited all the sister-lands from time to time. She relished his tales of far away places. His was a view very different from the sisters who embellished their own gardens sometimes beyond Heartland's imagination.

Heartland traveled too, but only underground, and although the essence of Sir Wind was everywhere there was breath (even underground), it was only during their visits on the face of the earth that he came with the company of himself.

Heartland and Sir Wind got along famously from the very beginning of time because she could take his blustery as well as his mellow self; always welcoming his many moods, and also because he brought change (mostly refreshing) and always fascinating news which stirred her dunes, her flowers, forests and stream to nature's music. To her, Sir Wind made her wildest flowers dance and her woods sing like no other instrument at her bidding. She was not one to show off, but the profusion of her flowers and leaves swaying at Sir Wind's command was a thing of dazzling joy. Sir Wind and Heartland did enjoy one another's company.

Lately, however, Sir Wind's stories of other places were becoming a bit disturbing. Heartland could not keep up with all the news; the tales, so preposterous, they scattered her imagination into complicated puzzles. She sometimes became quite overcome with wonder. There were so many things that she had never heard of, had never seen, had not even thought to think about! She found herself comparing her handiwork and her place on Earth, to all the different distant sister-lands, with their strange sounding features.

Even so, she did enjoy Sir Wind's stories and escapades. He would make her wonder, her eyes growing big with awe. But he always paid attention to her gardens, her pretty river, her new flowers, healthy trees of birch and elm and oak and pine. He even noted her onions that seemed to defy taming; they were growing wilder and wilder. Those onions insisted on growing wild and in great profusion despite Heartland's attempts to tame them.

It was Sir Wind that made her really appreciate all the effort she had poured into coaxing baby-nature-beings to become the marvelous birds and butterflies and fishes they were. And many times Sir Wind and Heartland would have happy talks all day and late into the night. They would occasionally end their musings by just laying back and gazing on the starry, moonlit heavens. It was Sir Wind that reminded Heartland that she was made of stardust. It was one of their favorite stories—the one that recalled how the Earth and all they knew came to be.

On this particular day, Sir Wind mentioned the new pine trees that Heartland was growing and she explained that they were evergreens. She told him that although she loved her four seasons, most of her trees turned beautiful colors in the autumn and then fell to earth to nourish the soil for future life. Their former life on the limbs of trees left the branches bare. She had received a new recipe for evergreens that stayed green and hearty even in the coldest weather of wintertime. She thought them a wonderful addition to her nature family.

Sir Wind was very impressed with her evergreens, but then he began one of his traveling tales. "Since the space of time when last we talked much has changed in the world." He paused, as though remembering something amazing. Heartland remained silent and waited for more of the news because she knew better than to rush Sir Wind. Then, in a short while, he went on…"Yes, much has changed just as you yourself have changed." He raised himself among the leaves of a nearby tree causing its leaves to dip and wave. "Look how tall your trees have grown and how strong your grasses, but would you believe that I have seen a fabulous ocean, far to the west that roars, and whose land is so fair she has trees with trunks that dance with me while their leaves bear husky, brown fruit that have sweet meat and milk inside them to drink!" Actually, Heartland could not imagine such things, but was too abashed to say a word. Sir Wind had uttered all these words in such a rush, she was momentarily speechless. Sir Wind went further as he continued to rustle the leaves, "This same land, with the ocean that roars and the trees that dance, doesn't have your four seasons. She only knows the summer time and..."

"Wait!" cried Heartland, forgetting her politeness, "What on earth is an ocean?!"

"An ocean", ruffled Sir Wind, for he did not like to be interrupted, is like a million, million rains that have fallen and stayed in one place, but not exactly—because its waters are not fresh like rain. An ocean is quite salty. The land there told me that this salt from the waters is of the utmost importance for other living things." Then he puffed, "and don't ask questions while I am talking!"

But it was too much. Heartland wasn't listening anymore. She was trying to imagine an ocean—a million, million rains!? She was thinking of trees with trunks that danced in the wind—that could make milk and sweet meats??! She looked at her westerly flanks and then down to her gently curving southerly slopes. She looked and looked at her vast plains and she began to feel a terrible sadness. Her trees, while strong and handsome, with branches that swayed, had thick heavy trunks whose roots would never allow them to dance with the wind.

Great tears began to roll down Heartland's face. They dripped in huge pools of sadness and went flowing down her easterly shoulder. Soon she was having a crying fit right then and there! She didn't care that Sir Wind was watching her. She didn't care one whit! She just didn't care at all!

"What's this!?" swhooshed an astonished Sir Wind, "a land who cries about wonderful things!?"

Sir Wind dashed around Heartland's head in big swooping circles. He hovered near her face which she was now trying to hide. He whistled and snorted..."An unhappy land and a mature wind do not mix!" With that he gathered himself into a puffy huff and went swooshing away and away some more. But Heartland cried and cried and only stopped long enough to whimper, "I wish I had an ocean and t-t-trees that dance with their trunks. I'm so plain, so plain, so very, very plain!

Heartland wept on into the night causing torrents of tears to slide continuously down the gentle slope of her easterly shoulder. By morning she had created quite a puddle that spilled all along her entire eastern side, almost to the sister-land that lay on the edge of Heartland's vast, treeless flats. She surmised that those tears would dry up soon and she turned her back on them and spent the rest of the morning sunning her self next to an onion patch while trying to forget Sir Wind's stories. She only began to find contentment when a little voice reminded her of Mother Nature's remedy for small annoyances: "You must flower to flourish. You mustn't flounder in fretting…!"

For a time things went well. Heartland, now busy with trying to control her onion patches that still preferred being wild and unkempt, was enjoying a glorious new Spring. As a matter of fact, this Spring time was rather special because "The Little Onion" (as she now thought of herself more and more) had just come through a very hard winter. During that cold time Sir Wind was ever present, but he was traveling so fast and was having such a fierce old time keeping his brothers, Swifty and Sweeper, from getting carried away, that visiting was simply impossible. Yet, there were some good times too, when Sir Wind would catch The Little Onion in one of her bare leafless winter trees. Then he would blow the falling snows into high mounds and hills, taller than her dunes. She would jump into the highest snow heap as Sir Wind swept across her frozen, icy winding river to the north. Oh, how the crystals of snow would whirl through the racing wind and sparkle in colors from the bright, bright sun. And one cold, wintry night The Little Onion and Sir Wind danced under a full moon as it shined on the frozen river until stars surrounded the moon above them in twinkling delight.

Now it was spring time again and The Little Onion felt she had grown up quite a bit. She had decided to appreciate her own lands with their spreading plains, little dunes, and great onion patches. She busied herself encouraging little wild flowers and sapling trees to reach for the sun.

This she was doing one fine day when out of the north came Sir Wind. It had been a calm day, with hardly an air current stirring. The Little Onion knew right away that Sir Wind was there for a visit and she was glad to have her old friend's company especially since she felt much more grown-up and accepting of her self. She settled in the branches of one of her trees and Sir Wind hovered in its barely quivering leaves.

Sir Wind began to tell The Little Onion all about his latest travels. He spoke of a place where his great elder lived; a place where the Grand-Old-Mere-Whisper-Of-A-Wind had been since the beginning of ever. The Grand-Old-Mere-Whisper-Of-A-Wind spoke in the softest sounds where his words caressed all who were near with gentle wisdom. Sir Wind said that the place where this great elder lived was far off in the Milky Way and that only the quietest world-winds were welcomed there.

"And when would you ever get quiet enough to visit the Grand-Old-Mere-Whisper-Of-A-Wind?!" asked The Little Onion, smiling. And Sir Wind showed The Little Onion how he had gathered himself into the most delicate of gentle zephyrs by making the leaves on the trees around them almost completely still. Even the birds in the tree branches and the tiny, but noisy insects stopped their chatter in wonder of the now stillness in the air. "Oh, when your currents are like this, I can hear such a silence and feel such peace that it makes me quite sleepy," remarked an amazed Little Onion. Sir Wind immediately bounced into a playful whirling motion and replied, "No you don't! It's your turn to tell me what you've been up to since last we met, and then I have news for you!"

And so, The Little Onion told her friend about the good things she had been tending such as the marshland near her river, where pussy-willows sang in harmony with big bull frogs all night long.

It was a good visit that day with Sir Wind sharing new wonders he had beheld during his travels—of great deserts that stretched miles and miles from inland to the edges of those oceans he had already told her about. The Little Onion thought a desert must be a wondrous thing indeed, but she did not long to have one of her own. That much sandy expanse, without a tree to break its surface did little to appeal to her. And she had quite gotten over oceans, thank you!

When Sir Wind drifted off for other climes, The Little Onion was content. She went to her largest onion patch and settled down for a long nap.

The season of Spring in those days was very much like Spring is now and so there were sunny days of cool weather and warm days that were, nevertheless, cloudy and rainy. Still, sudden changes in weather could be surprising. One morning, out of a sudden turn, came a tornado. It was flashing with lightening and smashing things all over the place. From its fury a whipping Sir Wind swooshed around The Little Onion and came to a thunderous halt. The Little Onion was quite out of breath as she ran around her grounds trying to keep her trees from uprooting and trying to tidy up fallen branches and dunes in disarray. She was very annoyed. "Just look what you've done to my fields and sapling trees! Chaos! Chaos! It will take a season to straighten out the tumbled jumble you've brought upon my lands!"

"Forgive me," sighed Sir Wind, and he flopped down on her startled grasses in a tired heap. "It's the unruly nature of my family, you see, and what am I to do but join them? Swifty and Sweeper started this storm as soon as they spied a bunch of dark clouds gathering south of here. They jumped in those clouds before you could blink an eye. They kicked up a terrible fuss and I had to join them before they went too far. Before I knew it, my tail-motion picked up so much speed I was barely able to slow down for this visit with you!"

He looked so tired and spent that The Little Onion forgot about her tussled, tumbled fields. She sat down beside Sir Wind and they listened to the ever new and beautiful music of the universe. It was always unusually pretty after a storm because the natural instruments of Mother Nature's orchestra—the rocks, leaves, flowers, animals, sands, clods of earth, waters, and such—had all become rearranged from the disturbance (finding themselves in new spaces way beyond their control), along with the birds of the air as well as the creepy, crawly things of the earth. This made their familiar composed music of Earth, after being involved with the storm, a new song and of course, the storm itself was a rousing, impromptu, song all by itself—naturally!

Sir Wind stretched his airy self into a contented murmur, "How sweet the song of life after so much rushing and pushing and jostling about!"

"Oh I do agree", said The Little Onion, "but tell me Sir Wind, what else, other than being a part of stormy weather, have you been doing since last we met? Have you spent any time with my distant relatives? I haven't been underground for a visit with my sisters for ever so long."

"Well", chimed Sir Wind, "you know me. I come and I go and I see many fantastic things between here and there and back again. Why, way north of here I've come across a land with colossal rock formations that reach so high they kiss the sky! Oh, what fun I've had soaring around their tops and in their nooks, their crannies, and their caves. There I've flown in the rarest airs and raced with the eagles." He paused, remembering, and The Little Onion sat very still, trying to picture those colossal rocks.

Sir Wind went on, "Some of those mighty rock formations are craggy or smooth with incredible designs. Some have huge forests of pines, like yours, and other varieties not seen anywhere else. The tops of these places stay dressed in snow while their bottoms bask in balmy weather!" Sir Wind stole a glance at The Little Onion to see how she was taking this news. He was not surprised to see her face framed in wonder with a small frown beginning to wrinkle her forehead. Satisfied that she was impressed, but quiet, he began to speak again. "These giants are called mountains and..." But, The Little Onion uttered such a mournful sigh that Sir Wind became distracted. Annoyed by her interruption, he snapped, "Whatever is the matter!?"

"I wish I had a mountain," cried The Little Onion, "I'm so flat and plain...so very, very flat and plain." With that, huge droplets of tears began to spill from her beautiful, but sad eyes. Those droplets formed big tears that ran down her easterly side again.

"What a mess!" howled the wind, and with that Sir Wind left in a rush almost as fast as he had appeared.

The Little Onion sobbed and wailed all night and by morning she knew that this time the huge lake of tears wasn't going to dry up. Much of her dunes had flattened themselves into a sandy shore around her lake of tears and refused to allow the growth of trees she had thought to fashion in order to hide those shameful waters. The lake seemed to be an ugly thing, because The Little Onion was ashamed of it and it reminded her of the way she behaved when she was miserable over things she didn't have and would never own.

The Little Onion looked around herself and thought, "Why It's the season of new life and creating new things and here I have been crying over other things that are wonderful even though they will never be on my earth. How silly of me! I've got lots and lots of things to do!"

She went through her fields and awakened drowsy baby buds into blossoms. There were violets and roses and sunflowers, impatiens, bluebells, daisies, and hundreds of onion patches just waiting for her attention.

She manicured her new wheat—not too tall and not too short. She made tree leaves greener and bigger than ever before. Then she swept her dunes into neat mounds and sprinkled her marshes with the nicest reeds and willows she had ever fashioned. She looked at her wild onions and created new varieties, trying to make them prettier in spite of their pungent odor. She was determined to be content with herself and not be a cry baby when Sir Wind came to visit again.

When she had finished her chores she gazed at her handiwork and felt a deep satisfaction. Then, just for good measure, she covered her wide, flat plains with more tall grasses and more flowers than they had ever known. Afterward, she climbed her tallest tree and looked at everything growing and glowing around her. She felt happy, but she was also filled with certain melancholia. She was feeling the first "spring-fever" on Earth. A kind of sleepiness came over her and she fell into a reverie that was full of shadow and dreams. Soon she was dreaming of the old days when she and her sisters lived with Old Sol…when they were part of the pure star of heaven.

The Little Onion dreamed of the letting go time when she became part of the new planet, Earth, and went spinning on the face of the deep. She recalled that one of the best parts of flying from the sun was being given all the instructions that came with the new beginning. For, besides becoming a planet, the Earth was told of its future.

In her dream, The Little Onion remembered that all this preparation, honing her small part of the new planet, was to be in readiness for the grandest happening to come: The First People. She settled right there, in her dream, for a long moment to savor what an exciting event would soon be a part of her very own essence, and that of all her sister-lands, maybe very, very soon.

Then her dream took her deeper into its sweetness and she realized, in a fresh new way that only dreams can bring, that she was part of the dust from a bigger dream; that the Earth of her life was truly made up of star sprinkles and that no star sprinkles could sail in the heavens without the winds. The Little Onion smiled in her sleep as she thought of Sir Wind.

When The Little Onion awoke next morning, she was grateful for such a good dream. It made her remember who she was and what her true purpose was on the earth. That good dream made her more eager to tend to her part of the Earth and to oversee all the beauty, new and old, surrounding her. Dreams, she thought, must be sent to us in our sleep to give us clues as to what we were doing and whether the things we were doing were right for us or being done correctly. Dreams, she realized, were silent teachers that came in the night as we rested from all our busy doings. Dream teachers gathered their lessons from our daily scurrying about during the day hours and then, when we are done with all our work and we give ourselves over to sleep, dreams come to teach us and, perhaps, delight us with new wisdom.

The Little Onion thought she would tell Sir Wind about her lake of tears. He was her best friend and she thought he would laugh with her over the silly business of her crying over things she did not have. She would tell him how she had grown, especially from her dreams, and how blessed she now felt because she better understood how Earthly things worked. She finally realized that she was blessed to have the special things that were hers to love and care for. She looked forward to his next visit. Perhaps they would ponder on all the different wonders of the Earth together without her being in the least bit envious or sad. In the meanwhile, she had work to do and she felt very happy to do it.

The next thing The Little Onion knew she was receiving a mysterious message about another underground gathering to take place with Mother Nature. She could never explain how she knew when these meetings were to take place, but all the lands knew, down to the very nature of their little grains of dirt, when it was time to race through the roots of their trees to Middle-Earth.

She centered herself in her favorite big oak tree and went down, down, down its intricate roots until she found herself in the beautiful and magnificent cathedral of Middle-Earth. It was good to see her sister guardians of the land and to listen to the musical sounds of their chatter. Jolly overtones noisily filled the deep earth's humid air with greetings and news.

When Mother Nature called them to attention, the sister guardians eagerly quieted themselves. Mother Nature looked out at her daughters of the land with pure love and then she spoke: "My daughters, when you go back to your lands today, you will find new residents from the animal kingdom. They have come to add their being and their stories to every corner of the world. They will serve many purposes to balance life on Earth. They will be food and clothing for some of the people to come, but most of all they shall live for the joy of living. Like all the creatures and natural things of your lands, they will always depend on you for life support. When your first people arrive they will have to decide how to live in harmony with the animals and among themselves. You must help the animals and the people. The Great-Grandfather Spirit has given you everything you need to provide well for all the creatures depending on you. You are able to give them good health and comfort. You shall cooperate with humanity even though they will try to tame and conquer you.

"My daughters, you have done well on your lands, creating beautiful gardens and perfect creatures to keep those creations working in harmony. You must always work with joy so that your creations thrive and do well. Now, close your eyes and just relax while the music of life pours all over you. And remember, in order to flourish, you must continue to flower!"

When The Little Onion got back to her lands, she was delighted to see huge herds of powerful animals roaming her great plains. They were munching her delicious grasses. There were horses with manes that blew about in the breezes of Sir Wind. There were skunk, wolves, moose, and deer. Lots of rabbits hopped around and they were amused at the little mice and moles who popped their tiny heads above ground every once in a while just to look around at all the wonder. Now The Little Onion had inherited a great four-legged family to enjoy her lands and rivers.

Sir Wind had a good time playing with all the new life on Earth and, of course, he came to pay a visit with The Little Onion before too long. The Little Onion was so glad to see her old friend and was even happier to see his delight over her new animals. She asked him about the animals living in her sister lands and Sir Wind excitedly launched into amazing descriptions of animals The Little Onion could barely imagine. He told her of tigers and mongoose, of lemurs and monkeys. He was in a flurry of whirling breezes as he traced images of exotic animals in the clouds above. The Little Onion was intrigued and not one fretful tear came near her eyes.

Then Sir Wind settled down and spoke of other news. In a kind of just remembered rush he asked The Little Onion if she recalled the mighty mountains he had told her about and of course she did recall those towering creations, but she was not prepared for Sir Wind's next revelation. He said that from some of these low-lying mountains—cliffs really—came thunderous, roaring waters that poured in non-stop happiness to waters below just for the fun of it! Sir Wind said these waterfalls were miles and miles long stretching along the edge of her sister lands! He said that waterfalls crashed and dashed and splashed all day and all night without one single pause! He said they were a symphony of sound and wonder all by themselves!

The Little Onion was absolutely dumbfounded. Waters that fell from cliffs all the time without stopping!? Well, it was too much, but she kept herself calm for the moment as she asked, "What is the purpose of these waterfalls?"

Sir Wind howled with laughter. "Purpose?" he repeated, "Why they're here on earth just to please the spirits of everyone and everything, but if you listen closely to their song, you will hear them sing of many things to come to ease the lives of the people of this planet. Their mighty powers shall be harnessed for a new kind of energy that only the people of Earth shall discover. And, speaking of people, the First People have arrived on two of your sister lands continents away. They are magnificent creatures, very curious and worthy of the sun itself." Before a stunned Little Onion could speak he added, "Compared to waterfalls, they are puny little things, but still they have a special knowing that is hard to ignore."

Listening to this torrent of information all at once was beginning to wear on the delicate nerves of The Little Onion and she was about to ask Sir Wind if he could fly somewhere else for a while, but he was on a roll and continued to share more marvels of the First People continents away.

"The First People in one of the continents have fashioned housing for themselves out of the trees. They have discovered golden rocks in the mountains and pretty, shiny rocks that glisten like snow that never melts. And, far away, on the North continent the First People make their houses out of snow. They love to laugh and have a remarkable relationship with the animals of their land. Their land is so cold I almost froze in my tracks during my last visit with them!"

It was after this long announcement that Sir Wind finally noticed The Little Onion's discomfort. You see, all the time Sir Wind was telling The Little Onion his stories of others lands he was flitting about in grand swooshing gestures; now in the trees, up high in the clouds, and back on the ground whipping up the gravel. "What's the matter" asked Sir Wind. "Don't you enjoy hearing about such wonders?" Sir Wind looked at The Little Onion suspiciously. "You're not going to cry again, are you? If you do, I am going to sail away like the wind I am in one big hurry!"

The tears began like a miniature waterfall of her own and before The Little Onion could pull herself together to muster up a response, Sir Wind said, "Uh-oh, I'm off!" and with that he left in a puff of a huff!

"Where are my First People", cried The Little Onion, "Why are they taking so long to get here? Maybe they like places with waterfalls that run in symphonic cascades better than they like flatlands!" And with that The Little Onion flooded an already teeming lake down by her easterly shoulder.

The Little Onion soon got over her crying spell and began to work hard, trying to make her lands more tempting for a First People to want to come live with her. She created wide expanses of prairie devoid of all but tall grasses that stretched for miles and miles. That prairie was like an ocean of waving grass that sang a soft song of gladness on the breezes of Sir Wind's relatives.

The Little Onion was pleased with her handiwork and marveled at the grand view from horizon to horizon. Never had the plainness of herself been seen as so grand. She felt much, much better about herself and that was good.

"Well," thought The Little Onion, "I don't have deep canyons that fall into the earth like upside-down mountains, and I don't have diamonds or mammoth waterfalls. I don't even have trees with trunks that dance or monkeys, but my prairies go for long, long ways in all directions. They reach over lands that are strong and straight. My earth is filled with fragrant, good-smelling black dirt that is rich and fertile. When my First People arrive I believe they will be happy to be here."

In the late spring her enthusiasm was quickly dimmed when only one lone fur trader settled on her river's shore. Of course she was glad for the miracle of him and was grateful that he had chosen to make her land his home, but other than his woman, there were no others. She knew, from Mother Nature, that all of the guardian lands should receive big families of people arriving together. Had The Little Onion been right? Was her land unwanted by clans and tribes? The Little Onion did her best not to believe this and she reminded herself in the weeks that followed how content the fur trapper seemed to be on her land. Nothing for her, thus far, appeared to happen in the same ways it did on her sister lands, but something new was happening inside her: She was beginning to enjoy being "different!"

Summer arrived in all its glory and The Little Onion was just visiting her winding river and her plains when all of a sudden Sir Wind flew in like never before. He rolled and pitched about. He lurched and whipped to one side. Then he rolled again, lifted, ruffled, buffeted and dipped down beside The Little Onion in a quivering roar of excitement—"Wheeeeeeooooooh!" he yelled, "come with me right now! I've seen your lake…and, wheeeeeeooooooh! Come, come right away!"

"Do not torment me" said The Little Onion. "I am not proud of that lake of sadness and I wonder you have taken so long to see it!" Sir Wind dipped down beside The Little Onion, who was sitting on a green leaf, floating on her river.

Sir Wind could hardly contain his excitement, but he said as gently as he could, "My friend I do not enjoy seeing you cry and I did not want to remind you of how that lake of yours came to be, but you must come with me because you have two new miracles today that include that very lake!"

Hearing this The Little Onion immediately wrapped herself into some loose onion skin--which had become one of her favorite ways to travel with Sir Wind--and quickly flew to the eastern shore of her land.

When they arrived The Little Onion found herself in complete amazement. There, on the great, great lake, her First People had arrived and were coming still in many fine canoes. The Little Onion was so happy. Now she understood that the fur trader was the first person, not the First People, to call her land home! Now they were here! She thought it was the best day of her life. She turned to Sir Wind and said, "This is a wonderful day and I already know the second miracle. It is this lake that I had accepted as my shame. It is not a shame, but the very vehicle that my First People needed to come home. All the time my tears were a gift from Almighty Creator and Mother Nature. I am glad I released those tears. If I had kept all that sadness inside, my lands would not have blossomed and flourished at all."

Sir Wind laughed. "Maybe that is a miracle and also one way to see the lake, but you are, in some ways, like your sisters: I have often brought their attention to new miracles they might not have noticed in more ways than one! You do know that news travels on the winds!" He smiled at his own joke.

The Little Onion was puzzled. "What else could be more amazing than my First People arriving by way of the lake?" Sir Wind danced in gales of laughter and The Little Onion, wrapped in onion skin, found herself tossed and blown about so much she decided to change her clothes to something more substantial! "Stop teasing me", she chided Sir Wind as she morphed herself into a big boulder, "and tell me what you know of another miracle."

"Blowing through your First People", Sir Wind began, "I heard them talk about this lake of yours. They have been watching it grow for a long time, but more than that they all agree that it is the best tasting, fresh water they have ever had to drink!" The Little Onion felt so humble and grateful because this news was the grandest of all. It did, indeed, prove she was right in her knowing that the lake was not a shame, but was one of the best parts of her life. She knew she would never doubt her own worth again and would always look for the good no matter how things around her seemed to others or to her own.

Sir Wind and The Little Onion spent the day watching and listening to the First People of the heartland. One of the first things they did was say a blessing for the land and then they explored the area. They expressed happiness over the vast prairies and the view from horizon to horizon. They discovered the winding river and made friends with the fur trapper. Then they talked with their elders about all the onions on the land. In the weeks that followed they found many ways to use the onions. It was onion soup that cured their children of sniffles. They used onion skins for poultices, and flavored many of their others meals with those pungent vegetables. And they laughed through their tears as they chopped and diced up those onions; for only and onion can make a body cry real tears without even trying!

It should be no surprise that the First People called their new home on the shore of the great, Great Lake, Chi-ca-go! It was that word that came to mean "Little Onion!"

Now this is a tale from my elder's elders and you can believe it or not. Some say Chicago means "Wild Onion" and some say ot means "Stinky Onion", but you can believe "onion" is a part of the translation. To give Sir Wind his due, many call Chicago "The Windy City", but that too, has many other tales. The Lake, however, has one more telling thing about it that you should know. It joins four other mighty bodies of water and they all reach wonderful shores. They say these "Great Lakes" formed from glaciers of ancient times. That may be so, but the one that touches The Little Onion is shaped like a giant tear!

The End.

LOVE

Most of the games created for the internet and television are overwhelmingly of violent content with scores of ways to murder opponents via a "joy-stick." Think of the glee and uninhibited "joy" exploding from game-players when they have vanquished a cartoon foe! Methinks we humans have been bamboozled toward a love of violence even as we take mental shelter under an ever shrinking cloak of peace (and oh, how we love simulated car crashes and the like!!)

I once heard a scientist say that the scientific world is made up theories and hypotheses; that life is made up of physical realities which stem from the grey matter in our heads; that love is only one experience of our grey matter; that free will is only a *sensation* of choice because physics is actually pulling the strings. He further said that God is a sensible idea, but not on the principle of making things happen beyond the realm of physical possibilities.

At that point I stopped listening because I realized this obviously intelligent scientist lived with a mind bent on proof outside the light of faith and that he did not know the heart-centered shadows of mind-boggling-bending mystery. His was a world of intellect and hard data. Mine was a world of gentle awareness and love's inscrutable power. I can't say there was room for me in his world, but mine definitely included him and every one else!

Too often we, of lesser education and experience, fall for the "big" words of seemingly bigger persons than ourselves. Spin doctors send messages to us of cleverly worded statements intent on making us responsible for our own financial problems as well as Earth's looming demise. Those truly (or mostly) responsible for disasters plaguing the world create dazzling skews on truth and sell them back to the citizenry wrapped in accusingly guilt-ridden clothes. The not so funny thing about that is how unquestioning we ordinary citizens buy big business' spin doctor drool! We literally eat that crap up!

I will never forget the "Americans are addicted to oil use!" In other words the oil barons are only trying to keep up with demand by production and because of that oil spills happen! How crass! We all know that Americans (particularly car owners) would use processed pee to drive their automobiles if it could be processed for that use and made available! If we citizens are addicted to anything it is getting ahead of the game and trying to manage greed. Those fat cats know this better than we do and use every trick in the proverbial book to keep us hooked and inches behind the dangling carrot! Sometimes these super-rich magnets put an impossible distance between themselves and the poor and use that distance to extract even more money from the general populace by selling studies of their lifestyles for the have-nots to have as keep-sakes to dream on. It is an on-going game of mammoth proportions. And the more the ordinary citizen dwells on (his) lack, the more (he) misses the opportunity to develop (his) own wealth, dream, and personal gifts—perhaps to be like his wealthy counterpart: To sell his unique offerings to the rest of the sleepyheads just like himself! Or (he) might uncover his personal gift as a means to further enlighten the masses. Unlike the aforementioned scientist, I see that we all have the power of choice in concrete abundance to use everyday, or not, as we deem fit--or we always have the option to give up our inherent right of choice out of appalling ignorance.

If internet game designers created pastimes where opponents vied for getting a valentine to a sought after lover before their rival achieves this aim without resorting to murder, they would lose their proverbial shirts today, but consumers are well-known for grabbing anything new, especially when the old attraction becomes unavailable. When the current toy loses its luster, consumers can be counted on to grab the new toy with all abandon. But games of peaceful pay-offs are less than desirable today because we have been programmed to believe it is more fun to kill one's opponent in order to win the game rather than use creative diplomacy as the means to end-game. Of course, the other course offered is to blow up everything between yourself and winning! We are ever being programmed for divisionism and war.

More and more the world populace is waking up. We are coming to understand that war and hate do not work in our best interests, nor do these negatives solve our problems, but we are very slow in acting on this new knowledge. Right does not necessarily control might as is obvious in the many nations gone to the streets in protest, so fed up are they from governmental maltreatment. People are realizing their worth beyond religious or racial differences. They know their own birthright is a manifestation of supreme respect whether they hold the reins of leadership on a grand scale or not!

The average citizen is no longer a helpless victim, but is coming into a spiritual power to be reckoned with. They are taking that power and self-respect to the very doors of their oppressors. Unfortunately, I have seen too much "joy-stick" reveling over a small gain that turns into rampant glee in wanting to physically punish a captured "dictator". Whatever happened to exile? We must fight against unwarranted punishment to those found guilty of crimes against humanity lest we become the oppressor in new clothes!

Many years ago I was privileged to take a spiritual journey to India. It was a most profound experience; one that I continue to learn from and cherish to this day.

In one of our daily lectures from our guru, we were given an eye-opening narrative on love. All my life I have known that love is the way to live a good life and is the open door to the way of peace on Earth. But I have also been painfully (sometimes) aware that love is not given much credence in media communication and is not taught outside the home at all except in homiletic offerings from church pulpits. Love is often scoffed about as the means of making saps of us and the daily news is mostly about money, even as the bottom line of some natural disaster. News of kindness and heroism are mentioned as asides beside the monetary cost surrounding events that affect (and assault) the senses.

I had come to India from a country where a song called, "What's Love Got To Do With It?" became a super-hit! Yet, I knew in my heart of hearts that love has everything to do with all there was to life. I remembered another title of a book by Erich Fromm, *The Art of Love*. The book's recurring theme is "love or perish." I was a young woman when it was released, but I was thrilled and knew it was an important work for human growth. Yet, it only made a dent in the pimple on the ass of progress!

After that lecture on love in India, I could understand how a scientist might perceive love as a mental experience. No one can control love, not even scientists, and without control many lose their grip on reality.

Love is a phenomenon of the heart—not the pumping vessel of the muscle in our chests—but a kind of vessel that carries us safely from the shore of the physical to the sublime.

Bhagwan (my Indian guru) said that when you fall in love you throw away your reason completely because falling in love constitutes a fall from the head to the heart! For some it is only a step up in consciousness coupled by an intense flowering of feelings. For others it may be like falling off Mt. Everest! Obviously science and modern man can't accept this. Modern man must have reason—must have control—must have logic! And love is not logical.

It is as though, in our modernity, we have condemned "falling in love" because the head, the reason, the intellect, cannot look at it without finding fault with it. We even laugh at it, but not in mirth or dear understanding. Rather, we laugh at the condition of "falling in love" in bad jokes and worse, often bitterness. This sad perception leaves us ripe for wrong direction and mental programming away from our natural need to love and to be loved.

Love is a rising, not a fault. With love you expand and become more than you were before. You don't shrink, though some, at the onset, may feel as if they were sinking into a frightful unknown. But fear and love cannot occupy the same space and the more you accept the love you feel, the less fear can invade your living.

If you feel love for another and you allow fear to overshadow that love, it is because you do not trust your heart. You feel out of control. But understand that this is part of the work of love. To fight against your fear and to practice embracing the love in you and its need to expand, to grow, to make you more alive, this is your new bridge to becoming more fully awake.

If the love you feel for another is not returned, you might feel emotional pain, but understanding that love given freely is always returned is one of the gifts and mysteries of recovery from unrequited love. Your heart may be broken, but as it heals the broken part gets stronger. The only requirement on your part is not to give up on love.

Understand that love is a free agent. When you are in love with the universe and romance becomes part of that equanimity, you already know that your beloved is a whole unique being of infinite possibility just like you. If a person returns your love you are immensely blessed, but if they spurn your love, let them go. Let them be free. Silently bless them on their way. They may return. It may be too late, but in any event you know that no one possesses the other—EVER. Both the lover and the beloved belong to love itself and are only able to share their particular measures of that wonderful stuff. Jealousy and possession do not make good bedfellows with love. Jealousy and possession smother love, extinguish the fire that energizes and uplifts lovers. Never bring those dimensions into relationships of love.

The link between us being connected by love is a beautiful thing, but it is just that—a link. No other is your "other half". You are a whole being as is the other. Love between two persons is the catalyst that blooms between you as you cheer each other on to greater heights and better things. Love encourages the beloved to soar, to grow, to be more of the best of themselves. As you practice this with your beloved, you also grow and become more alive and happier.

And one more thing about nursing a broken heart—always be good to yourself. Do really nice things for yourself; get massages, volunteer at a soup kitchen or a children's hospital…read to children that are going through battles you could not possibly understand. Give them your loving kindness. Nurse your broken heart by mending the hearts of others. Practice smiling until it becomes a new habit. Soon you will find yourself on a higher plane of love than you were before and before you know it love will find you again.

Instead of looking for love, let love find you! How do you do that? By being a loving human being; by being a blessing in someone else's life. It is so easy, it is profound.

Love is patiently waiting for you and me to become an us as in **united selves!** Of course nature is not so patient as is evidenced by the havoc being leveled all over the world. It is in direct association with the karma resulting from man-made greed.

Souls, more prolific and wiser than I, have warned us ("Love or Perish"), cajoled us ("Love Makes the World Go 'Round"), have supremely sacrificed for us (Jesus) and given us thousands of heroic efforts in proof of love's healing and grace, but we are incredibly slow to take these lessons to heart long enough to run with them in harmony and a lasting peace. There are examples of loving kindness happening every day, everywhere, all the time. Let us energize that truth more and more. We must, if we are to survive. But our attention is purposely focused on the evils that be rather than the good that is. In this 21st Century we should not have to be **reminded** to be kind to one another and to be gentle with ourselves first and foremost. These **powerful** tools are another part of our spiritual DNA—Divine Natural Attributes—that we do not energize nearly enough. Let us correct that!

Our era, our so-called "civilization", has shown itself to be as false and as inhumane as all its former historical eras put together. We have finally created weapons of mass destruction and brought ourselves to the brink. We are sadly out of time, out of sync and out of balance with peace. We have come to the edge of destruction, but do not be deceived: Earth is in the process of healing itself and will do so, even if (she) has to get rid of us in order to survive!

We have the power to overcome the looming demise of this world. Our world is not the Earth. Our world is that space we have created upon the Earth. We, as a people, are weapons of mass salvation. We are magnificently made and we have many diverse cultures, and many religious paths on the **same** road to paradise. We are different in so many ways and we speak many different languages. With all these differences it might seem normal to be ill at ease with those outside the "norm" of our preference and upbringing, but we are put here **TOGETHER** for a higher reason than the treason of cutting ourselves away from all that is not familiar. Besides that, we are much more alike than we are different: No matter what language we speak, all our vowels evoke the same responses; all our emotions reveal the same connections; all music, painting, sculpture, dance, drama, comedy, etc. transcend our disparities. We are on this planet together to embrace one another in brotherhood; to share our beliefs, to share our discoveries and our wonder. We are one family with many different components. Together we can conquer all negativity and join our new-found humanity with the highest evolution possible.

Today the people of Earth have spoken. Equal rights, justice, respect, fair and equitable government, freedom, and peace are the demands of humanity all around the world. The only sane war left to us is a **combined war against disease** of the physical body, the mental body, and the spiritual body. Let us combine our intellects and our hearts to that single purpose as we take our true and *ultimate* place among the stars.

I MESSED UP GOOD, BUT I GROWED OUT OF IT

I spurned many a prince

In my day,

But oh

The frogs with whom I swooned

Now

That's

A

Tale

With

Warts to spare!

GLOWING

I saw a rainbow go through

My body bold

It raced on a second of

Timeless gold

I felt a rainbow sing

Through my soul

Oh lo and behold

That second made everything

Rhyme whole

And tho one second so

Fleeting was it

That I moved with the pen in my hand

I'll never never ever forget

That instant spent

A rainbow ago

When I saw what I felt in me.

A BIT OF COSMIC CONSCIOUSNESS

I believe there are other worlds in other galaxies teeming with life and distinct possibilities, but I am an Earth-bound transplanted spirit, housed in human form, trying to make it real where I am.

Today, there are open and closed debates on the question of extraterrestrial life. These debates run hot, cold, and rampant. The probabilities are tremendous in scope and unproven--(?) logic.

I recall that famous line from Carl Sagan's book, "Contact": "It would be an awful waste of space if Earth is the only life in it." It is one of those simple statements that make profound sense.

I submit that before we Earthlings can approach or appreciate the question of looking for extraterrestrial life, communicating with (it), or publically disclosing its existence, we **must** resolve the differences among ourselves by accentuating the positives, eliminating the negatives, and dispossessing the demons within and between us, peacefully.

Only then will we **earn** the right to inter-galactic exploration as well as other stellar evolutionary treats.

NO MORE HATE

Now hear the word of the servant of God—Obadiah: Chapter 1, Verse 15: "For the day of the Lord is near upon all the heathen: as thou hast done, it shall be done unto thee: thy reward shall return upon thine own head."

This past week (ending June 29, 2015) nine human beings were brutally murdered as they worshiped in church (Charleston, S.C.—USA); Twenty-seven believers were massacred as they worshiped in their mosque (Kuwait, Persian Gulf). Seven African-American churches have been torched in the United States (ostensibly in retaliation for a new ban against flying the confederate flag. Only one of those burned houses of God has been confirmed an "accident.")

Israel and Palenstine war with one another; Kosovo simmers with divisionism; Russia wars on the Ukraine; China bedevils Tibet; "gangbangers" kill for insane initiation in their own neighborhoods. Children are starving in every "civilized" nation on the Earth—even here in the USA! Desperate people cling to unfit craft on dangerous seas (often losing their lives in the process) as they try to reach shores of a (hopeful) haven since living in their own lands have become more dangerous than the decision to risk death. Some reach another country only to be housed in camps with filthy conditions or are sent back to their unwanted fate. Practically every nation on Earth is diseased with hate.

Regarding the confederate flag, no ban would have been necessary had the progenitors of its worth as a symbol of Southern heritage been truly honest about that heritage. Then the flag would surely have been lowered in solemn respect for those African-American families mourning their slain loved-ones because the proud heritage of the South is a direct "gift" of Black women, men, and children! It was Black folk who made cotton king. It was Black folk who produced the sugar-cane, tobacco, and rice whose profits filled the coffers of white men. It was Blacks, brutally treated who, even-so, grew the food, prepared it and served it to whites. Black women suckled white babies. Blacks actually helped the white man in every way imaginable to achieve wealth and position including his self-worship! It was Black hands who made the very bricks that became great edifices that stand against the sky to this day. Why then, is there such hate for this, one-time, unpaid servant who gave so much to make this country great? What have Black people done to deserve so harsh a resentment? There is no intelligent answer to this question!

Hate is a terrible disease. It has an insidious nature that literally eradicates logic and reason. The honored French author, Voltaire, wrote (almost 300 years ago) "Prejudice is the reason of fools!"

In time-honored tradition, the families of those murdered Christians spoke to the murderer in court about their pain and anguish resulting from his crime, but they then said they forgave him. They slashed through their grief with the sword of truth and the balm of Gilead.

And then our President, Barack Obama (who happens to be an African-American) became an even greater President by delivering a eulogy of unprecedented beauty for slain Reverend/State Senator Clementa Pickney. It was unusually beautiful because it obviously came from his heart. He sloughed off the cloak of politics and inspired a grieving nation as he soothed our rattled senses with words about "grace." That grace came alive with a kind of healing electricity. His eulogy ended with atomic shock-waves that still reverberate around the whole world as he sang "Amazing Grace." He didn't leave Charleston before visiting every family mourning a loved-one from that single violent act of hate.

Shortly afterward, our Vice-President, Joe Biden, put aside his personal sorrow and went to Charleston also to give solace to the families who must bear this awful burden the most. Without media fanfare he showed up and worshiped with some of the family members. We are truly blessed at this time in history to have leaders unafraid to be human and humane at the forefront of their lives.

But we must remember, as my dear mentor reminded me, that "forgiveness is a process." It is like a bridge made of rope. It sways, it rocks, and every physical motion is reflected in trembling courage. It causes crossing feet to be mindful of each and every step in order to become spiritually true. Getting to the other side of that shaky bridge is the moment true forgiveness takes root. Negotiating the bridge to complete and lasting forgiveness is partnered with what the heart has decreed. There will be times of unbearable anger and disbelief; we are only human. But being human *and a believer* allows the humanity of righteous anger to flow in easement right back to mindfulness.

I propose an end to hate. America could become the TRUE greatest nation on Earth if it introduced a new **Required Course** in every public school that teaches **TOLERANCE**.

What a standard-bearer of peace we would be! This course should begin in pre-school and reinforced all the way through college, as well as in the home.

Babies should be made aware that they are precious; that while they are precious, so are their playmates, classmates, brothers, and sisters. They should be taught that they will not always agree with one another, but learn to solve their differences and squabbles **without** violence.

Elementary and high school students should be made to understand that we are a world of many races, cultures, religions, and political arenas: That while one may truly believe their way of life or worship or looks, are the best way to be and/or live, their way is only *ONE* way; one that is right *for them*. Yet even as they accept their rightness, it should be suggested that they take the high-road of tolerance for others—even if they perceive those others to be *wrong*. "Bama," a New York poet, said, "Everybody has a right to be wrong except judges and presidents. With so many lives in their hands, they have no right to be wrong!" Of course we must also teach and understand that on our way to tolerance, being judgmental (without the mantle of the arbitrator) is a very precarious business only to be used with much care and thought (and as little as possible where others are concerned). It should be used in times of prudence where proper judgment begets charachter of self. Those times where one has to question whether they should carry out a specific act is mostly best left undone! This is how wisdom begins and where the positive character of self grows and evolves.

Tolerance produces RESPECT. Respect for self and for others is the Atomic Balm much needed on our planet.

To all haters: I pray for your deliverance and healing. Please remember, and know, that hate is not the opposite of LOVE. The opposite of hate is PEACE. The opposite of LOVE is indifference. If you cannot tolerate those unlike you, your indifference woudl be more than welcomed on your way to inner-peace.

To everyone: Look again at the photo of Earth taken by the Hubble telescope. Behold our sacred place in space and let your hearts be glad.

Peace,
Bonita

GUN FEVER

If only Newtown had been unprecedented news;

Something we could collectively rule a never-again-occurrence!

Alas, the Connecticut event only takes its place

At the end of a long and vicious line

Connected to very sick spirits

Wielding guns

Totally

Out of control and out of sanity.

It is an issue

That is leaving humanity

Out of prime time.

AFTER THE TORNADO

After the tornado I tried not to see the glee

Of those abused souls

Whose own stuff

Stayed put

While the local haters bore the brunt

Of the angry wind.

There is no justice or discrimination in tragedy—

Can't they see?

Bad things definitely happen

To bad people

And we all know

The good suffer religiously on Earth!

So, what's the use,

I ask my tired self,

But knowing the answer better than most

I release the ghostly host of

My heart;

I open my heart and let it

Haunt the world at large

With big, new doses

Of old, old love.

THE SANDS OF LUXOR

What is this presumptuous familiarity coursing

through my body

from the bottom of my bare feet

to the crown of my head?

I am made ten years old again

with my happy toes kneading the sands

on a beach in Chicago.

But I am far, far from the lake

that I have loved since youth

and I am not ten, but fifty and ten

and new to Egypt.

How can it be that this music on the

evening breeze pierces

my heart like a "Bird" solo

when these ears know not this song?

Why this heady aroma of laughter softly

floating to shore from a sailboat

gliding by on a mystic river

that kissed my fingers just yesterday?

How can I know so well

what has not been my acquaintance?

And what is the source of this

irritation when I cannot decipher

the handwriting on the wall

as though I had forgotten how to read?

Am I beguiled, seduced, or merely unmasked

by my African roots

rerouted to a timeless truth?

BLESSED

Happiness moving on wings

Of fortune smiling and

Love's impeccable touch

Makes me wonder

How we can deserve so much

When we are groping thru

The dark of this day's comeuppance

And such as it brings

With time in tow

for

I am lost in blessings

As I ever was in strife

And that be the truth of it,

If the truth be told.

For the time is now—

It always is,

Yet I keep trying to tell it

Apart from itself

Even when my heart

Takes flight

Over some unforeseen light

Come to wake me

A bit.

And when the ride

It takes me on

Slows down

I quit the place without

A trace of longing.

For I have learned

One thing,

And that is this:

'tis wrong to count the

Teeth of gift horses

Or the ways of God.

I'LL NEVER BE THE SAME IS AN EVERYDAY REFRAIN

(For Ameen)

When you left, without so much as a fond fare-thee-well, my soul felt the freeze of a naked chill. Of course death does not honor the living's formalities or other predictable pronouncements. Yet, how could I know it would, or could, steal my will?

Was I prepared then to join the ranks and small swell of women whose men had left them both deeply grieved and strangely satisfied? No, I was not; but here I am with lust at bay and a brand new day dawning on my spirit's dignity…all without my permission or proclivity.

I have thanked your visiting in ghostly aura a hundred times over, but damn man— what have you done!?

I am made undone in this life-oven that warms my mortal frame with coils of time from a light grown dim in my heart; a half-baked sweet am I, perchance to be reheated in the drama of well-done love confections. But, I doubt it.

How suspicious I've become of love's auspicious penmanship since you slipped quietly away from this particular lifeline.

Where before, in youth, it did not matter how the ink of fate turned my head, these latter years of wise and true retread render both my mind and my heart a toddler on spindly legs trying to traverse the landscape of no escape.

Still, I am at home in splintered pieces of peace--so sweet and so familiar--I am soothed even in the lonesome evidence that missing you proves to be. And so, I tarry in my new and welcoming residence here on Elder Avenue without undue complaint, thanks to you and Jesus and mama.

BLACK MAN

(Dedicated to my father, Stephen McCall III And all the men of color who knew how to play the game in our favor without instructions.)

You made the Nile blue again.

Kilimanjaro's majesty is your presence.

You are the rhythm of mother Earth.

The sun is released in your smile.

Lake Victoria dances in your eyes.

You are older than Africa

And

Younger than the beginning.

The Sphinx secret lies just behind your frown.

The vitality and grace of the gazelle

Are you.

The regal stealth of the panther

Is yours.

Astute and aloof,

You can only be reached by

Your permission,

For there must be proof of punch in the pudding offered.

If not,

You prefer the knot that might ensue.

Goodness is your most familiar other

And your heart is held in sacred trust

Ordered by the most "Mus' Is"

'cause "mus' ain't" don't sound right!

You have been captured by life,

But your soul cannot be conquered.

Origin of man become flesh,

You remain fresh to this day;

Imitated by design and stealth

While your wealth grows way beyond markets, bytes, and

Paper bills.

You are energy flowing and flowing energy

Resounding, bounding, and reaching for itself.

Your spirit is contagious

And

I love you, Black man.

OBSERVATION #9

Time is only a man-made

science fiction continuum

imposed upon us in order to

make human sense out of

God's

perpetual NOW!

UNTITLED

I have lived for love and understanding,

Yet learn I do from other source and light.

Those latter lessons in my mind do cling;

They've healed a wounded heart and gave me sight.

Love is still the greatest boon of my life;

I follow it with seeker's soul to know,

But now I do not think of me as wife,

Instead the love is all I need to grow.

It glows within; it dances on my walk.

It moves, like lightening, thru my laugh and tears.

It's in my prayer, my speech, and all my talk.

It colors all the sequence of my years.

Even things that once would have erased me

Wisely bow before love's proximity.

THE GOOD LIFE

The good life is

A puzzle

Living through you--

There

To

Solve itself

Piece by peace.

OCTOGENARIAN CONCLUSION

Being an elder has its good side, like coming to the realization that it is very wise not to waste time while I take my time.

I've come to the conclusion that I really have all the time in the world even as I reckon time is running out. I'm the sand in the hour-glass, slipping through the purposeful crack. The sand is still in evidence when it reaches the bottom; resting there until the cosmic Hand that runs the cosmic clock tilts the hour-glass of my existence down-side-up one more time.

And though I have said it before, I think it bears repeating: Time is only a manmade chronological continuum in order to make human sense of God's perpetual now.

Finally, I suggest that it is good to keep on smiling as an active practice; to be a loving person as much as is humanly possible, and to always look for laughter in the equation. Otherwise, at this juncture, what's the point?

AFFIRMATION

(Veena Bonita's Vision)

Love it.

Truth prevails.

Justice is alive and moves beyond manipulation.

All wars – that kill – have lost their meaning and their thrust;

Their weapons become powerless, their weapons misfire and fail all direction.

Hate has lost its strength.

Its stranglehold on humanity becomes a weak and pitiful thing.

Violence has lost its strength too, and finds no work available.

Let all governments, everywhere, yield to the people

For the people's benefit first and foremost –

For what are governments, but people?!

Let the citizens be aware of their power and not misuse it.

The Earth is healing right now.

The awakened universal consciousness moves with us,

Surrounding all naysayers, doubters, and other usurpers

In a circles of extreme light.

Their energies are quickly sent out of Earth to a safe harbor to be

Nourished back to health

Because

Love is!

Truth prevails.

Justice is alive and moves beyond manipulation!

Power to all the people who practice **being** human;

They increase in love, compassion, super-consciousness, humor,

Purpose, powers of forgiveness, humility, numbers, courage, vision,

Spirit, and heart.

They attain, retain, and sustain radiant health

And abundance according to God's riches in Glory

Because Love reigns supreme.

God is Love.

Love is **Life's Oldest Vibrating Energy!**

And so it is this day on planet Earth,

Located on a blue island

In the Cosmic Sea

Of the Milky Way Galaxy.

EPILOGUE

Dear Reader,

Love… This book is an invitation for you to re-visit that astonishing photo of Earth taken from outer-space. Study it. Wrap your head and heart around the fact that this is the ultimate photograph of you as in "us", as in "we", as in wheee!! And you will expand in knowledge on many levels. You will grow.

The photograph of Earth touched me in places I had not known were waiting to be stirred to life. I felt much more alive just looking at it. It kept dawning on me that this is where I live! This is where I am right now! It was more than a "wow" moment. I marveled in wonder because I am a part of this beautiful, round, blue, marble-looking vessel out here in the vast sea of space. I recognized that we are just hanging out here, not tethered to anything except man-made logical physics and the utmost magic of mystery! It humbles me; makes me feel minute in an immense kind of way.

Way before I saw the photo of us I knew we, as human beings, were one species; one family on this planet. Whether we like one another or not, the fact remains that we are all related as one entity living among a multitude of other living beings. I knew that Earth, itself, is a total living being and a miracle that we have yet to completely comprehend. We are part of this living vessel – this sailing ship of saints and fools and other evolving souls. The photo only served to expand and confirm what I already knew: We Earthlings are supposed to be here for a greater reason than mere existence. We are here to find a way to co-exist in a viable, lasting peace. I believe humans were placed here as (another) experiment of LOVE: One that has the never before "mix" of many races, ethnicities, cultures, religions, and individual levels of consciousness, all thrown together like a bag of mixed nuts, expected to be **GOOD together!** We are challenged to do this by the grace of God through our collective willingness to save our home planet. Then we stand to gain exponentially on many fronts in exploration, discovery, invention, and most of all in evolutionary love. We are here to achieve this through the same stuff that brought us out of total ignorance: **Life's Oldest Vibrating Energy!**

The photo of us also confirmed one other thing for me about the mind of our Creator: **God is crazy about circles!** You have no idea how this revelation affected my consciousness from the thousands of tiny, tight, perfect circles that make-up the hair on my head (now in "locks" I love that I once despised as "ugly naps"!), to the stars I was taught to draw as sharp, five-pointed things rather that the circles they actually are! When we look at the sunset, we see a big orange colored CIRCLE or "ball" on the western horizon. Our sun is a star! Stars are circles, just like my hair (that I was tacitly taught to hate), just like our Earth, like all the other planets, and the asteroid belts, and so on and so on… ad universal! What a connection of incredible worth clicked inside my brain and my soul! Like Freddy, from Leo Buscalglia's *The Fall of Freddy the Leaf,* who saw the whole tree for the first time when he finally found the courage to let go and fall off the limb where he had lived his whole life, I marvel at the sight of our world in all its glory. I marvel and I praise our Creator for blessing us with this reality – the real view of our selves without a single one of us in sight!

We are not designed or meant to be Narcissistic. The human body has eyes on the front of its face; eyes that look outward, ahead of itself so that we see where we are going. We can also look back and see where we've been, but we cannot see our own faces or the back of our bodies with our own eyes! Could the reason for this be so simple as to make us understand that we are to look at ourselves from the inside out? We grow and find fulfillment from looking inward. When looking at ourselves, other than for the purpose of grooming, our best view of self comes from wrestling with and working with our inner selves.

No one has ever seen their own face except as a reflection, and no mirror is 100% accurate in the image it gives! Yet we are obsessed with our faces! In far too many cases, how one looks to another is more important than anything else we assess about the other. Content of character is rarely more significant as a first impression. This conceit has grown all out of proportion in meaning and has given rise to a kind of insanity, a basis for all sorts of unfair divisionism, hate, and unwarranted disgust! But where are all the pretty human faces in the cosmic photo of our beautification? Like us, the planet was not designed to show off its parts or the special features of itself from an appreciable distance!

Every body is a beautiful creation of subtle perfection whether that body leaps, limps, or does not meet someone else's standard of physical attractiveness. As Sly and the Family Stone once told us in a song: "Everybody is a Star!" How true.

Dear Reader, this book is an invitation for you to celebrate your self – your life, and your oneness with all creation.

I like to remind myself of the positive contributions of African-Americans as a non-competitive race among all the races "running" things on Earth. One of the most magnificent creations from Black people is the only original music to come out of America – jazz. This art-form turned the music world upside down and inside out! It created rhythms and chords that defied category or definition, but that also worked in positivity, healing, and enjoyment inside the human being. In its inception, jazz was in turn denigrated and highly praised and imitated. It was a gift of collective joy and goodwill. The unique qualities of jazz fired the imaginations of people all over the world and also lifted the spirits of all who embraced it.

This music came to life out of suffering and from the beauty of being able to find love and humor in spite of that suffering. It was born of grace from a great and benevolent God who saw fit to deeply bless a new form of humanity in a new land being re-formed and re-discovered.

Many other inventions came out of the Black experience in America from medicine and heart-surgery, to the ironing board; from the peanut to the traffic light! But the new music called "Jazz" became an ambassador of friendship whose connections broke through color barriers. Jazz heralded in a new age of enlightenment. It healed the disease of hate. Jazz was, perhaps, the second weapon of mass salvation on Earth. I think Christ Jesus was the first!

One other phenomenon unearthed by jazz is the essence of being "cool." When one becomes "cool" one if more than "laid-back." Listening to the music, one is unruffled to the point of being "hip" – enthused and imbued with the "sounds": Sounds redefining all areas of one's life beyond the accepted status quo. The music tells us what's really happening in a kind of telepathic way and when it hits us with the uncontested truth between our ears, real life is deciphered all the way down to YES!

Sometimes the music of jazz is a truth so deeply accepted that the listener has to silently holler about it as though he, or she, has just gone to church! Its lessons strike home and plant a refreshing clarity in the heart. And we take the lessons that jazz imparts back to the streets, to our homes, to the job, to the romance in our lives. We color our personal dreams with the sounds, or maybe we find our personal dream for the first time rising out of this "cool" music that thrives on keeping us surprised.

The composition of jazz resonates with all that is natural as well as the political times of the moment. Being "cool" means that one has learned to adhere to one's HEIR CONDITIONING: That noble estate passed down from African roots to slavery in America, to the abolishment of that sick institution, to overcoming Jim Crow, to going beyond hate, to the inimitable jargon of jazz master, Lester "Pres" Young, to the pearly gates of "free at last" without the necessity of death.

The "cool" movement came out of jazz because the music is rooted in natural truth. It seeks out the ironies of life, the tragedies, and the fun. It is basically a happy sound, but it never, ever runs away from what is there before it, be it fair weather or foul, chaos or life's endearing miracles.

Better than this revelation is the knowledge that some of the hippest people on Earth are "Squares!" (Something my dear brother, Stephen, "hipped" me to a long time ago!) This understanding turned me on to the benefits of jazz as a healer. It helped me recognize that I was more than a Black woman, more than a definition, more than an individual. It made me see others in much the same way, with respect for their right to be the way they choose to be. And if I perceived them to be "wrong" in any way, I was made aware that everyone has a right to be wrong, including me. The music we call jazz makes forgiveness and awareness a very sweet experience.

I have learned that the "I" of me is ego, but the "aye" of me is the evolved willingness of my spirit to sail in concert and in oneness with all there is and ever will be as long as love is involved.

I therefore invite you, dear Reader, to embrace yourself fully: Your culture, your contributions to the betterment of mankind, your religion or non-religion, your art, your anger, your enlightenment, your healing, your stories, your individuality, your laughter and tears, your gifts. Share what you will, but embrace yourself fully. Embrace yourself with the wholeness of your oneness with the circle of life. May you come fully alive and fully awake in a newness of spirit and find yourself in perfect harmony where you are, as you are. May you always consciously dwell in life's oldest vibrating energy on purpose.

PEACE,

BYM

ABOUT THE AUTHOR

Bonita Y. McCall is a self-professed, life-long student of the ways and means of Love: Its constancy, the on-going surrender, the unconditional aspect of the ideal, its healing powers, and the human struggle to let it be. She lives for the evolution of humankind's collective heart-center to become as important a force as is the world's focus on mind and intellect. She firmly believes this is at the core of Earth's salvation.

Bonita is a mother and aunt, a friend, a world-wide traveler, poet-writer, lover of art in all its forms, and a classically trained pianist. She is a native Chicagoan, but currently makes her home in North Carolina. She has one other published work: "Car-Car's Journey – A Story for the Child in You."

www.ingramcontent.com/pod-product-compliance
Lightning Source LLC
Chambersburg PA
CBHW080606090426
42735CB00017B/3355